Louis L'Amour

Twayne's United States Author's Series

Warren French, Editor

Indiana University, Indianapolis

TUSAS 491

LOUIS L'AMOUR
(1908–   )
Photograph courtesy of Bantam Books, Inc.
©*1985 Leigh A. Wiener*

Louis L'Amour

By Robert L. Gale

University of Pittsburgh

Twayne Publishers • Boston

Louis L'Amour

Robert L. Gale

Copyright © 1985 by G. K. Hall & Company
All Rights Reserved
Published by Twayne Publishers
A Division of G. K. Hall & Company
70 Lincoln Street
Boston, Massachusetts 02111

Book Production by Lyda E. Kuth
Book Design by Barbara Anderson

Printed on permanent/durable acid-free
paper and bound in the United States of
America

Library of Congress Cataloging in Publication Data

Gale, Robert L.
   Louis L'Amour.

   (Twayne's United States authors series; TUSAS 491)
   Bibliography: p. 140
   Includes index.
   1. L'Amour, Louis, 1908–   —Criticism and interpretation.
2. Western stories—History and criticism.
I. Title.   II. Series.
PS3523.A446Z67   1985   813'.52   85-8627
ISBN 0-8057-7450-5

To the memory of

my mother, Miriam Fisher Gale (1887–1984),
and my father, Erie Lee Gale (1885–1979):

born in pioneer Nebraska and Minnesota,

knew the Western experience,
but blessedly never read a Western novel
in their lives

Contents

About the Author

Robert Lee Gale was born in Des Moines, Iowa, and was educated at Dartmouth College (B.A.) and Columbia University (M.A. and Ph.D.). He served in the United States Army Counter-Intelligence Corps in Europe during World War II. He has taught at Columbia, the University of Delaware, the University of Mississippi, and the University of Pittsburgh, where he is now professor of American literature. He has had Fulbright teaching fellowships to Italy and Finland, and has also lectured in Germany, Canada, Denmark, and Russia. Gale is the author of *The Caught Image: Figurative Language in the Fiction of Henry James; Thomas Crawford, American Sculptor; Plots and Characters* volumes on Henry James, Nathaniel Hawthorne, Herman Melville, Edgar Allan Poe, and Mark Twain; the Henry James chapter in *Eight American Authors* (revised edition); Western Writers Series booklets *Charles Warren Stoddard, Charles Marion Russell,* and *Will Henry/Clay Fisher;* and study guides, chapters and articles in reference works, critical essays, and reviews. Gale is the author of the TUSAS volumes on *Richard Henry Dana, Jr., Francis Parkman, John Hay, Luke Short,* and *Will Henry/Clay Fisher (Henry W. Allen).* He teaches courses in American literature, especially nineteen-century fiction, Civil War literature, the Roaring Twenties, and Western literature.

Preface

Louis L'Amour looms like a uniquely living dinosaur on our literary horizon. Look toward the West, and you will see his long shadow. He is not merely the best-selling writer of Westerns who ever lived; in addition he has probably outsold the next ten or fifteen combined. His publisher crows that there are 145,000,000 copies of L'Amour in print. Moreover, he is one of the four best-selling authors now alive. Finally, unlike most of the other top sellers, he does not include smoldering sex scenes; also, his vaunted Western violence is tame by comparison to that of most popular Western, detective, police, and spy fiction fashioners.

L'Amour is known to his loyal millions first by his popular and frequently appearing paperback Westerns, which seem almost to crowd off the racks the works of such other worthies as Zane Grey, Max Brand, Ernest Haycox, Luke Short, Jack Schaefer, A. B. Guthrie, Jr., Will Henry, Clay Fisher, Elmer Kelton, Will Cook, Gordon D. Shirreffs, Ben Capps, and Matthew Braun, all of whose literary merits equal his. But he is also known to millions through movies made from his fiction, most notably *Hondo, The Burning Hills, Heller in Pink Tights, Shalako,* and *Catlow*—not to mention made-for-TV items such as *The Sacketts.* Nor does L'Amour hesitate to appear on TV himself, both as colorful guest and as hawker of his own wares. Further, in 1983 President Ronald Reagan decorated L'Amour with the National Gold Medal that Congress had voted him, and a year later the president bedecked L'Amour with the Medal of Freedom. Finally he struck for respectability by going hardbound: *The Lonesome Gods* (1983) and *The Walking Drum* (1984) both achieved unprecedented status by being on best-seller lists for many consecutive weeks.

L'Amour is an anachronism. He succeeds just the way Mother's Day, apple pie, baseball, Chevys, and Ronald Reagan do in these otherwise dyspeptic times: he extols the old-fashioned American virtues of patriotism, loyalty, unflinching courage, love of family, and a vision of the Old West both as the arena of the famous American second chance and also as mankind's last, best hope. All these elements may be corny, but they still ring true to the consuming public and thus sell well.

Although he was born in 1908, L'Amour is still going strong, and has recently even branched into the medieval European, Middle Eastern, and Oriental fictional and philosophical scenes. Further, he has announced that he might soon try writing some space fiction. After all, space is the ultimate frontier, and L'Amour defines himself not as a Western writer but as a frontier storyteller. He has almost fifty unfinished books on his rough-hewn drawing boards right this minute. More power to him!

In chapter 1 of the present study I sketch in broad strokes the life of Louis Dearborn LaMoore, better known as Louis L'Amour. In chapter 2 I show the range of his long fiction, discuss whether it is mainly formulary or historical, show its diversity with respect to place and time, and touch briefly on his short stories—Western, nautical, and detective. (I cannot even hint at the contents of L'Amour's 400 or more pieces of short fiction, which have not been and never need to be collected.)

In chapters 3, 4, and 5 I move chronologically through L'Amour's astonishing parade of novels, and do so with two main points in mind. First, from the start L'Amour seems to have shown a genius for writing what his public wanted; so he shows rather too little variety from about 1950 to the late 1970s. And second, he seems to have been aware that he was building more and more fictive structures with mainly old building blocks and, therefore, tried manfully to introduce new features where he could. The results are often successful, but sometimes the new architectural elements are merely gargoyles or odd windows a little askew. Chapter 3 concerns the fiction from late 1949 through 1959; chapter 4, 1960–70; and chapter 5, 1971 to the present. (Having to stop somewhere, although my energetic subject seems determined never to do so, I have chosen wonderful 1984 as my terminal date.)

Perhaps L'Amour's greatest accomplishment in literature will prove to be his sagas of the Sackett, Chantry, and Talon families in the New World over a period of three centuries. Accordingly, my long chapter 6 concerns these sagas alone: writing in which L'Amour has implicitly invited comparison with other writers of long series having historical backdrops, recurring characters, and Zolaesque family trees. L'Amour also seems to require critics to point out some of his characterological and temporal problems and inconsistencies.

Such difficulties are not the only ones that beset an author like L'Amour, who is entirely too fast and facile. Hence, in chapter 7 I attempt—with no disrespect whatever—to put on record his alarming stylistic infelicities as well as to point out manifold excellences in his handling of setting, character, structure, diction, and sources (both literary and historical). In this same chapter I also discuss L'Amour's major substantive obsessions: Indians, women, and advice-giving (on many subjects). Since L'Amour is still at work and possessed of undiminished creative energy, it seems inappropriate for me to offer a conclusive chapter.

Still, I may add here that it is with immense pleasure that I acknowledge friendly sources of encouragement, advice, and information of various sorts: Henry W. Allen, better known to Western buffs as both Will Henry and Clay Fisher, who offered wise and witty counsel at many turns; Mary Louise Briscoe, chairman of the Department of English at the University of Pittsburgh, who provided travel funds enabling me to visit L'Amour's hometown, Jamestown, North Dakota; David Brumble, Pitt colleague and expert on American Indians; Clarence Decater, book collector, Roseville, California; Linda DeLowry-Fryman, Pitt's English Department bibliographer and a devotee of Western literature as well; Daphne Drewello, librarian at the Alfred Dickey Library, Jamestown; Richard W. Etulain, History Department, the University of New Mexico, expert on Western history and literature, and in addition an extraordinary bibliographer; Jack Evans, Jamestown journalist and a personal friend of L'Amour; Warren French, critic and patient editor; Brian Garfield, Western author and filmmaker, Sherman Oaks, California; Bill Gulick, Western novelist and long-time friend of L'Amour, Walla Walla, Washington; Reese Hawkins, friend of L'Amour and formerly of Jamestown, now of Greer, South Carolina; Lillian Jansen, secretary to the president of Jamestown College; Candace Klaschus, L'Amour expert from New Mexico and now teaching in Basel, Switzerland; Keith Kroll, Western-literature expert, Department of English, University of California at Davis; Savoie Lottinville, long-time friend of L'Amour, and former professor of history and university-press editor, University of Oklahoma; Edwin W. Marrs, Jr., Pitt colleague and fellow admirer of the Western spirit; Michael T. Marsden, academic friend of L'Amour, Bowling Green State University, Bowling Green, Ohio; Lt. Col. (ret.) F. E. "Bud" Murphy and his wife Jennifer, long-time friends of L'Amour and residents of Jamestown; John D. Nesbitt, Western literary critic, Eastern Wyoming College, Torrington; Carol and Cheryl Peuser, twin attractions at the Jamestown Information Center; Glenora E. Rossell, expert and generous librarian, Pitt; Annabelle LaMoore (Mrs. Rod) Shindo, L'Amour's knowledgeable and loyal niece, Omaha, Nebraska; Adeline R. Tintner, free-lance critic and friend, New York City; Edna LaMoore (Mrs. Frank H.) Waldo, L'Amour's knowledgeable sister and family historian-genealogist, Danville, California; Dale L. Walker, editor and friend, University of El Paso, Texas; and Mary F. (Mrs. Ernest) Young, Jamestown's informal historian.

Robert L. Gale

University of Pittsburgh

Chronology

1908   Born Louis Dearborn LaMoore on 22 March in Jamestown,
        North Dakota; seventh and youngest child of Louis Charles
        LaMoore, 1868–1952, and Emily Lavisa Dearborn LaMoore,
        1870–1954 (other children: Edna May LaMoore Waldo,
        1893–; Charles Parker LaMoore, 1897–1954; Yale Freeman
        "Bill" LaMoore, 1899–1954; Emmy Lou LaMoore, 1901–19;
        twins Clara and Clarice LaMoore, 1903–4).

1920   Part-time job as Western Union messenger boy.

1923   LaMoore family moves to the Southwest. Louis discontinues
        school, works as cattle skinner in Texas, hay cutter in New
        Mexico, circus hand in Arizona and Texas, then sailor to
        Liverpool.

1924   Continues in variety of knockabout jobs in Southwest and else-
        where in America, at sea, and in Far East (for years).

1926   Celebrates eighteenth birthday in Shanghai.

1939   *Smoke from This Altar*, first book (poetry).

1942   Enters army. Teaches winter-survival techniques, Michigan; in
        tank-destroyer and transportation corps, France, Germany; to
        first lieutenant; honorably discharged 1946.

1946   Begins writing Western fiction; settles in Los Angeles.

1950   Publishes, as Tex Burns, first of four post-Clarence Mulford
        Hopalong Cassidy novels (last in 1952); also publishes as Jim
        Mayo; *Westward the Tide,* first Western novel signed Louis
        L'Amour.

1953   Publishes *Hondo* and signs contract with Fawcett for one book
        a year; movie *Hondo* released (starring John Wayne).

1955   Signs contract with Bantam for two books a year (later altered
        to three a year).

1956   Marries Katherine "Kathy" Elizabeth Adams at Beverly Hil-
        ton, Los Angeles, on 19 February, honeymoons in West Indies
        and South America (children: Beau Dearborn L'Amour, born
        1961; Angelique Gabrielle L'Amour, born 1964).

1960   *The Daybreakers* (first Sackett novel).

1967   Lectures at University of Oklahoma annual professional writing conference.

1968   Meets Princess Margaret during royal premiere of *Shalako* in London.

1969   Wins Golden Spur award for *Down the Long Hills.*

1971   *North to the Rails* (first Chantry novel); appears on Merv Griffin show.

1972   Receives honorary doctorate in literature from Jamestown College, Jamestown, North Dakota.

1973   32,225,000 copies in print.

1975   Outsells Bantam's previous paperback best-selling author by surpassing John Steinbeck's 41,300,000 copies; *Rivers West* (first Talon novel); on *Today* show.

1976   On *60 Minutes* show.

1977   50,000,000 copies in print.

1978   Awarded the Great Seal of the Ute Tribe.

1979   *The Sacketts,* TV mini-series.

1980   Tours country for three weeks aboard Bantam's rented bus, as part of celebration of 100,000,000 L'Amour paperbacks in print.

1981   Wins Western Writers of America Golden Saddleman award.

1982   Voted National Gold Medal by United States Congress (awarded by President Ronald Reagan 1983); 120,000,000 copies in print.

1983   *The Lonesome Gods,* hardbound, on *Publishers Weekly* best-seller lists for nineteen consecutive weeks.

1984   Awarded United States government Medal of Freedom; *The Walking Drum,* hardbound, on *Publishers Weekly* best-seller lists for nineteen consecutive weeks; 145,000,000 copies in print; on *Today* show.

Chapter One
Life of L'Amour

It is different in the case of Louis L'Amour. But who cares about minor details in the personal lives of most twentieth-century authors of popular Western fiction? After all, such stories are usually cast back in the nineteenth century before those authors were even born.

Does it matter much, for example, that Henry W. Allen exercised polo ponies for Hollywood's idle rich? That James Warner Bellah served in the United States Army in Poland after World War I? It is not very helpful to learn that Walter Van Tilburg Clark was born in Maine and taught English; that Frederick Faust preferred medieval romantic literature before he became Max Brand et al.; that Zane Grey combined dentistry and baseball for a time; that Ernest Haycox was a soldier before making a hobby of collecting rejection slips for sea fiction. Yes, and Dorothy Johnson was a stenographer, an editor, and a teacher; Frederick Manfred was the tallest basketball player in the 1930s; Clarence Mulford was a civil servant and a librarian; Conrad Richter considered the ministry and was then a bank clerk and a salesman; Jack Schaefer studied Latin and Greek and was employed in a prison; Frank Waters was an engineer concerned with oil and telephones; and versatile Owen Wister was a musician, banker, and lawyer before that first trip to Wyoming.[1]

But L'Amour's case is surely different. Everything L'Amour did, before he turned to writing Western fiction, seems now to have been in preparation for his destiny—to become the most popular writer of Westerns the world has ever known. As with Herman Melville, Mark Twain, Henry James, Theodore Dreiser, and Ernest Hemingway, among a hundred other writers, it would now appear that just about every experience in all of L'Amour's varied jobs, locales, and ports of call became or is to become grist for the whirling mill known as Louis Dearborn L'Amour.[2]

Early Life

In January 1946 neophyte writer and ex-army officer Louis L'Amour went to a party in New York also attended by copy-hungry editors and publishers, one of whom heard that L'Amour wanted to write for a living and invited him to send Westerns to his pulp *Texas Rangers* and *Thrilling Ranch Stories*. The most phenomenal career in this pop-art form was thus born.

But this career did not emerge full-blown. Rather, it had a long background.

L'Amour is happy to trace his American ancestry back to the 1630s. He is also proud to note that in his veins runs English, Irish, French, and Canadian blood; and he is also pleased to follow his wife's English and Scottish roots far back. In fact, he points out that both sets of ancestors lived once in the same small town of under three thousand population and must, therefore, have known each other. Both families thus resemble his intertwining fictional Sacketts, Chantrys, and Talons, concerning whom he has said this: "As they move westward in different generations they brush elbows with each other and intermarry over a period of 40 years. In the end all their fates will be woven in together and in the course of writing these books I plan to tell the whole story of the West."[3]

L'Amour often mentions with relish the pioneering, fighting spirit of his forebears.[4] His paternal grandfather was born in Ontario and married French-Catholic Angelina LeDoux from Montreal. That man, Robert L'Moore, changed his name to Moore when he migrated to the United States, fought in the Civil War, and took up land in Michigan. Family tradition has it that the L'Moores (perhaps also spelled Larmour) were French Huguenot refugees in Ireland before migrating to Ontario. Robert L'Moore's son Louis Charles LaMoore, the future novelist's father, was one of twins (born 29 February 1868) but lost both infant sister and mother early to death, and was then reared by paternal grandparents in Ontario. He studied veterinarian medicine in Mitchell (now South Dakota) and Toronto.[5]

One of L'Amour's great-grandfathers on his mother's side was Ambrose Truman Freeman, an antislavery Virginian who moved to Illinois and then after service in the Union army during the Civil War went on to Minnesota, in time to fight against the Sioux and be killed and scalped by them on 24 July 1863 near the present location of Pettibone, North Dakota.[6] Another antecedent of L'Amour on his mother's side was Harvard-educated Levi Dearborn, an American Revolutionary army surgeon from New Hampshire, whose son Levi, Jr., moved to Pennsylvania. That man's son was Abraham Dearborn, who migrated to Minnesota and fought during the Civil War until his Union regiment surrendered at Murfreesboro, Tennessee.[7]

Ambrose Freeman and Abraham Dearborn later met on the Dakota-Minnesota border when they were both skirmishing with the Sioux. Freeman later introduced young Dearborn to his daughter Elizabeth "Betty" Freeman in St. Cloud, Minnesota. The young couple were married in July 1864 in Illinois; and a long time after that their third daughter, Emily Lavisa Dearborn (1870–1954), became the mother of Louis L'Amour.[8]

It was in Jamestown, North Dakota, to which Abraham and Elizabeth Dearborn had moved in 1884, that Emily met Louis Charles LaMoore, who went there from the little Dakota town of Ellendale about 1890. The two were married in 1892. After six older children, two of whom died in infancy and a third as a teenager, the vigorous couple welcomed Louis to the family. L'Amour's siblings, in order of birth, are Edna May LaMoore Waldo (born 1893), Charles Parker LaMoore (1897–1954), Yale Freeman "Bill" LaMoore (1899–1954), Emmy Lou LaMoore (1901–19 [died during the influenza epidemic]), and Clara and Clarice (twins, 1903–4).[9]

Louis Dearborn L'Amour was born on 22 March 1908. For some reason he likes to be vague, evasive, and secretive about his age. Perhaps it is vanity. He certainly looks young and vigorous, given not only his years but also his hard early life. Perhaps he thinks, as Edgar Allan Poe did, that if he knocks off a few years people will regard him as having started his literary career sooner than he actually did. At any rate, he told one reporter, "I spent my first years making people think I was older than I really was; now I'm working just as hard at keeping people from guessing my age."[10]

When L'Amour was still a child, his parents welcomed into their home a New York City orphan named John Otto, who had been sent west on a train with other unwanted Eastern kids. Feisty youngsters from crowded Eastern cities in L'Amour's fiction may well owe something to little Jack, who supplanted Louis as the youngest of the LaMoore clan.[11]

Doc LaMoore was a veterinarian for the state and in private local practice as well, was chief of police in Jamestown for a while, and taught Sunday school in the Methodist church. He was also a local juvenile commissioner, and served as a town alderman and as a county and state delegate for the Republican party, and was also a local park planner. He did business with and knew well many Indians in the region. He was sturdy, athletic—he taught his three sons to box—temperate, and colorful. His daughter Edna recalls that he "was passionately fond of horses and dogs and raised both."[12] As horses gave

way to tractors for farm work, Doc LaMoore began to sell steam thresh-
ers, soon finding himself able to repair such implements. Emily
LaMoore, L'Amour's mother, had studied at the normal school in St.
Cloud, Minnesota, wanted to become a teacher, but married instead.
She is remembered as a quiet person, a passionate gardener, an avid
reader, an amateur poetess, and a splendid storyteller.[13] L'Amour obviously inherited a combination of physical strength and intelligent
sensitivity from his marvelously matched parents.

From his earliest years L'Amour was an unusual blend of Huck Finn-
like physicality and Tom Sawyer-like bookishness. He attended school
faithfully for about six years but decided at the age of twelve that doing
so was interfering with his education. Thereafter, although he continued attendance until he was fifteen, he preferred both the outdoors and
eclectic reading, not only in his family's 300-book home library but
also hungrily in the local town library.[14]

A partial list of L'Amour's favorite reading, gleaned from many
sources, is as follows and is quite revealing: Honoré de Balzac, Edward
Bulwer-Lytton, Geoffrey Chaucer, Charles Dickens, Feodor Dostoev-
sky, Alexandre Dumas, Zane Grey, O. Henry, G. A. Henty, Victor
Hugo, Robinson Jeffers, Jack London, Henry Wadsworth Longfellow,
Karl Marx, Guy de Maupassant, John Stuart Mill, Edgar Allan Poe,
Sir Walter Scott, William Shakespeare, Robert Louis Stevenson, Leo
Tolstoy, and Anthony Trollope—especially O. Henry, Maupassant, and
Stevenson, for their technique. Later, L'Amour found his favorite life-
long reading, however, in Western diaries, journals, newspapers, and
history books and essays. It is as much a mistake to regard L'Amour as
a rugged outdoors type who does not read much as it is to say that
Ernest Hemingway, because of his adventuresome life, was not very
literate.[15]

And now back to the youth of L'Amour, who, when he was fifteen
years old, knew nothing of the famous Roaring Twenties. Indeed, in
many areas of America, especially in the Midwest, the average family
experienced hardship at the least and ruinous economic depression at
the worst. The LaMoores, as they agreed to call themselves beginning
about 1920,[16] were no exception. With the inexorable advent of farm
machinery, veterinarian Doc LaMoore found himself in straits. So he
and his family, in December 1923, sold out in North Dakota and
moved, first to the Southwest, in search of new opportunities. Young
Louis soon decided not be a burden on the family and struck out,
irregularly at first, on his own, returned to his parents again, and left

again, soon beginning to hold an incredible sequence of educative jobs.[17]

Harold E. Hinds, Jr., prefaces his fine essay on L'Amour with a careful summary of his subject's varied early career:

During the Depression [actually 1923] he quit school when he was 15, and by the time he was 19 he had skinned cattle in Texas, lived with bandits in Sinkiang and Tibet, and served as second mate on an East Indian schooner. Over the years he tried his hand at a wide variety of picaresque occupations, among them professional boxer, longshoreman, lumberjack, elephant handler, fruit picker, hay shocker, gold prospector, and tank officer during World War II. In short, he was a jack-of-all-trades, and self-reliant man who could survive on any frontier. As L'Amour expressed his view on the frontiersman: "In a land that demanded the most of an individual, what mattered was whether you could fix a wagon wheel, shoot food, ride a horse, shake a hand and make it good."[18]

This critic leaves little to add. However, an interviewer, repeating some items but augmenting the record valuably, comments thus:

L'Amour hopped freights, boxed in many prize fight rings, spent more than a few nights sleeping in jails, earned breakfast money handling circus elephants and eventually went to sea. He jumped ship in China where he knocked around the Far East in the days of the warlords and Japan's first military campaigns against its nearest Asian neighbor, living with bandits in Tibet and Sinkiang.

When World War II erupted, L'Amour was told he would be placed in navy intelligence where his knowledge of the Far East and Oriental languages would be useful. Instead, he found himself in Army khaki [drafted?]. Eventually he was made officer of a tank destroyer, and he finished up the war in Europe after fighting ashore on D-Day by commanding a platoon of the "Red Ball Express," the legendary unit of oil tankers that barreled along behind [General George S.] Patton's armor, bringing up the fuel the cavalry brigades gulped down to keep advancing.[19]

The years between L'Amour's leaving home and leaving the army were thus varied and exciting, with more than enough adventure to fill a trio of lifetimes. But precise details are lacking and will remain so at least until L'Amour finishes and publishes his promised autobiography.[20] Looming large in such a work would be L'Amour's being taken for a horseback ride by Buffalo Bill—he "smelled slightly of bourbon and tobacco"[21]—learning to box as a teenager and later doing so for money,[22] meeting famed old Bill Tilghman, observing, and then emulating his marksmanship,[23] and details concerning his relationship with his parents and siblings Edna, Parker, and Yale. An accurate account of his maritime and military service would also be welcome. And he ought to explain why, like novelists Nathaniel Hawthorne, Herman Melville, and William Faulkner before him, he too changed the spelling of his last name.[24]

But even without the L'Amour autobiography, a tidbit of additional information turns up here and there. For example, the sketchy and perhaps romanticized record can be filled in a little with the following data. When L'Amour skinned cattle in west Texas, he worked with an oldtimer who had lived with the Apaches and had known some of their great leaders. When L'Amour cut hay, he did so partly in Lincoln, New Mexico, and worked with two oldtimers who had known Billy the Kid. When L'Amour returned from sea, he associated quite informally with certain writing teachers and other people at the University of Oklahoma, in Norman, broke into print as a book reviewer, and gathered some of his randomly published verse into his first book, called *Smoke from This Altar,* now a collector's item.[25]

Beginning with the publication of *The Broken Gun* in 1966, Bantam Books, L'Amour's happy publisher, has made it a practice to include a page in the rear called "About the Author," in which still more of their favorite writer's exploits are revealed. Thus, we read, L'Amour "has lectured widely, . . . studied archaeology, compiled biographies of over one thousand [now up to 2,000] Western gunfighters. . . . He's . . . sailed a dhow on the Red Sea, been shipwrecked in the West Indies, stranded in the Mojave Desert. He's won fifty-one [fifty-four in some versions] of fifty-nine fights as a professional boxer and pinch-hit for Dorothy Kilgallen when she was on vacation from her column. Since 1816, thirty-three members of his family have been writers."

After the War

In 1946 L'Amour decided to live in Los Angeles and become a writer of Westerns—at that time and for a variety of reasons the most popular reading fare with the American public, which also had a voracious appetite for Western movies as well, and, a little later, for Western television series.[26] L'Amour was prepared to cater to that need, and the public was eager to make him a multimillionaire for doing so.[27]

At first L'Amour tried only routine Western short stories, with pulp publishers and then slick ones, including *Argosy, Collier's,* and the *Saturday Evening Post.* More than fifty such stories have been reprinted in the following Bantam collections: *War Party* (1975), *The Strong Shall Live* (1980), *Buckskin Run* (1980), *Bowdrie* (1983), and *Law of the Desert Born* (1983). These stories originally date mainly from 1946 through the 1950s. During this early postwar period, L'Amour seems not to have been certain that Westerns should be his unique metier. He was writing hardboiled detective fiction as well, as evidenced by the eight such tales collected in *The Hills of Homicide* (1983), which reprints material first published in pulps in 1947–52. A word may also be added here on L'Amour's *Yondering* (1980), a mixed bag of short stories of adventure in war and at sea. Better left uncollected, these fifteen weak pieces are mostly dated 1938–41 on the verso.

In 1950 L'Amour published his first Western novel, and did so, strangely enough, in England. It is *Westward the Tide,* which quickly dropped from sight, although it is a commendable work and introduces several themes central to an understanding of the later L'Amour. We find a curious diffidence in the early L'Amour, who published four Hopalong Cassidy books through Doubleday from 1950 through 1952, under the pen name Tex Burns. He also published *Showdown at Yellow Butte* (1953) and *Utah Blaine* (1954) under yet another pen name, Jim Mayo.[28] The less said the better about the quality of Tex Burns's writing; but *Showdown at Yellow Butte* and *Utah Blaine* are respectable action novels, especially the latter.[29]

Then L'Amour published "The Gift of Cochise" in *Collier's* (5 July 1952).[30] Its success was the turning point of his entire career. A year later L'Amour expanded its crisp, fresh plot into the novel *Hondo.* The publisher, Fawcett, ballyhooed it skillfully, printed 320,000 copies right off, and catapulted their author to fame at once and over to Bantam soon thereafter.[31] The fiction was quickly turned into a movie starring John Wayne, Geraldine Page, Ward Bond, and James Arness. Oddly, L'Amour sold the film rights for a mere $4,000.[32]

Promoting L'Amour

Hondo is the best-selling novel by L'Amour, who is the most phenomenally selling Western writer of all time. *Hondo* leads his hit parade with sales as of 1983 reaching 2,300,000 copies. His *Sackett* and *Flint* follow, with over 2,000,000 each. Then come *Silver Canyon, The First Fast Draw, The Burning Hills, The Daybreakers, The Sackett Brand, Mojave Crossing,* and *Lando*—just under 2,000,000 down to a mere 1,650,000 each.[33] According to Bantam publicity, all 82 of L'Amour's novels are in print and each has sold over a million copies. Total sales figures are astonishing: by 1973, 32,225,000 copies. Two years later Bantam crowed the news that L'Amour had surpassed their previous best-selling author in paperback, John Steinbeck, whose 41,300,000 copies now mean nothing compared to those of their new leader. In 1977, 50,000,000; 1980, 100,000,000; 1981, 110,000,000; 1983, 120,000,000; 1984, 145,000,000. Cocky Bantam avers that they now ship to stores all around a minimum of half a million L'Amours a month and have an unusually low return rate—only 12%.[34]

In 1980 one of the most garish gimmicks in publishing history was put on wheels. It was "The Louis L'Amour Overland Express," a 1972 Luxury Custom Silver Eagle bus, complete with master bedroom, sitting room, refrigerator and sofa, TV and stereo and Betamax, all leased by Bantam from an outfit in Nashville, Tennessee, which normally seeks its clientele among country- and rock-music stars and bands, not mere writers. During three weeks in June, L'Amour endured the tortures of cruising thus from Chicago to Moline, East Moline, Rock Island, Davenport, Des Moines, Omaha, Kansas City, Tulsa, and Oklahoma City—all to hawk his fictive wares, meet fans, and sign copies of his seventy-five titles then available.[35]

Meanwhile, moviemakers had not been idle. From 1953 when *Hondo* was first screened, through 1971, the sixteen best of more than thirty L'Amour-inspired films are as follows: *Hondo,* Warner's, 1953; *Four Guns to the Border* (source unknown), Universal, 1954; *Treasure of Ruby Hills* (from a short story of that title), Allied Artists, 1955; *Stranger on Horseback* (from a short story of that title), United Artists, 1955; *Blackjack Ketchum, Desperado* (from *Kilkenny*), Columbia, 1956; *The Burning Hills* (based on the novel), Warner's, 1956; *Utah Blaine* (from the novel), Columbia, 1957; *The Tall Stranger* (based on "The Showdown Trail"), Allied Artists, 1957; *Apache Territory* (from *Last Stand at Papago Wells*), Columbia, 1958; *Guns of the Timberlands* (from the novel), Warner's, 1960; *Heller in Pink Tights* (based on *Heller with a Gun*), Paramount, 1960; *Taggart* (from the novel), Universal, 1965; *Kid Rodelo* (from the novel), Spanish, 1965; *Hondo and the Apaches* (from "The Gift of Cochise"), M-G-M, 1967; *Shalako* (from the novel), Cinerama, 1968; and *Catlow* (from the novel), M-G-M, 1971. The star-studded movie *How the West Was Won*, M-G-M's 1962 Cinerama epic, began as James R. Webb's screenplay, which L'Amour later converted into a long and complex novel, published a year later. A series based on *Hondo* was produced and telecast in 1967–68. In 1979 a TV mini-series called *The Sacketts* was based rather closely on L'Amour's first two Sackett-saga novels, *The Daybreakers* and *Sackett*. In 1982 *Cherokee Trail* appeared on TV, and so did *The Shadow Riders*, based respectively on novels with those same titles.[36]

L'Amour is highly popular abroad. Commentators from 1972 on have revealed that he has been translated into somewhere between ten and twenty foreign languages so far. Interviewers and biographers have listed the following: Chinese, Danish, Dutch, Finnish, French, German, Greek, Italian, Japanese, Norwegian, Polynesian, Portuguese, Serbo-Croatian, Spanish, and Swedish. Without a doubt, L'Amour has supplanted Zane Grey, Max Brand, Ernest Haycox, Luke Short, and Henry W. Allen as the most popular American Western novelist in the eyes of foreign readers.

Personal Life and Present Success

L'Amour married relatively late, after his career as a highly paid Western writer was solidly established. On 19 February 1956, in a glittering ceremony in the grand ballroom of the Los Angeles Beverly Hilton, he wed the former Katherine "Kathy" Elizabeth Adams, who voluntarily discontinued a promising career as an actress. The marriage was the first for each. The couple honeymooned in the West Indies and on the northern coast of South America. Of his marriage L'Amour ecstatically says, "That . . . is when I *really* struck it rich!"[37] The L'Amours have one son, Beau Dearborn L'Amour, born in 1961, and one daughter, Angelique Gabrielle L'Amour, born in 1964.

The present L'Amour home in Los Angeles is regularly described glowingly by guests and interviewers. It is a rambling, Spanish-style adobe hacienda located on a quarter-block off Sunset Boulevard, and is complete with shaded patios and colorful gardens, a covered pool, a huge living room with fireplace, hallway, and study wing. This area includes a workroom with a high ceiling lighted by a rosette window.

Interiors are decorated with Indian rugs and paintings and dolls, mounted longhorns, original paintings first used as covers for many L'Amour best-sellers, a portrait of the author, and hinged double shelves for thousands of books, and even an adjacent gymnasium.[38]

L'Amour's seven-day-a-week, semispartan regimen includes early rising (say, 5:30 a.m.), an infallible six-hour stint at one or both of his two electric typewriters, then—if production has proved satisfactory (five or more pages per day, thus at least thirty-five pages per week)— a lunch with friends, regularly at the Polo Lounge in the Beverly Hills Hotel, and then a workout at the punching bag and with weights.[39] L'Amour boasts that he does not rewrite,[40] which is both obvious and regrettable. He lectures widely, travels tirelessly—in Canada, Europe, and the Far East, but mainly in the United States—to find new historical material and revisit beloved old locales, and even scouts scenes afoot with backpack, by four-wheeler, and by airplane and helicopter— recently with his son Beau as cameraman.[41]

Age cannot seem to wither L'Amour nor practice stale his ambitious plans. One interviewer in 1979 was rude enough to suggest that time had been taking some toll on L'Amour: "His bulwark of a chest has caved only slightly into his belly, and his six-foot [6' 1"?] frame is unbent despite its nearly 70 [seventy-one then] years of wear."[42] Back in 1973 he expressed the hope that he would sell 40–60,000,000 books in the next decade. He did so, and then some. In 1980 he announced plans for forty more Sackett, Chantry, and Talon novels.[43] Two years after that, an interviewer saw and commented on L'Amour's bulletin board, which was festooned with scribbled ideas for "at least forty-five . . . novels in the making."[44] Given the man's track record, can anyone doubt that he will fulfill this promise? He is insatiable in his hunger for readers. He told an interviewer this: "There are at least 25 million readers out there that I've never touched at all . . . and I want them—I want every damned one of them."[45] To another he commented, "It's nice to think when you are flying in a plane and you look down there and see the lights, you can almost bet that somebody is reading one of your books. It's a nice feeling."[46]

A facet of L'Amour's pugnaciousness came to the fore in the summer of 1983. At that time the New York publishing firm of Carrol & Graf announced plans to issue two collections of early short stories by L'Amour. All of the pieces were in the public domain through their author's negligence in not recopyrighting them. L'Amour filed suit in federal district court in New York. After some messy hearings, Carrol

& Graf were allowed to proceed, but only on condition that they alter their advertising and promotional material, and also the cover art of their two paperbacks, entitled *The Hills of Homicide* and *Law of the Desert Born*. Meanwhile, L'Amour had ordered Bantam to rush into print his "authorized" anthologies of the identical sets of stories (with the same cover titles), plus a few extras, plus prefatory and annotative material very hastily assembled. L'Amour properly had the last word, and Carrol & Graf asseverations of injury ring hollow.[47]

And now for two more pleasant notes. First, ever since 1962 Bantam publicity has reported the following: "Mr. L'Amour is re-creating an 1865 Western town, christened Shalako, where the borders of Utah, Arizona, New Mexico, and Colorado meet. Historically authentic from whistle to well, it will be a live, operating town, as well as a movie location and tourist attraction."[48] The world "shalako" as Shalako, the hero of L'Amour's novel *Shalako,* explains to the heroine, is the "[n]ame of the Zuni rain god. Seems like [he adds] every time I showed up in their country it rained, so they called me that for a joke" (*Shalako,* p. 17).

An interviewer in 1973 added the following details concerning the proposed town:

Sandwiched in between his writing for a few years now has been a pet L'Amour project that he hopes will be completed in the next year [1974?]. He is part of a multi-million-dollar investment in acquiring land in Colorado 11 miles west of Durango, where there is still an old narrow-gauge railway. The aim will be to set up an authentic Western town (circa 1865–1886) after the fashion of Colonial Williamsburg or Old Sturbridge, and to have it both a tourist attraction and possibly a site for filming movies. The Durango project, which will be called Shalako, has been mentioned in news stories and L'Amour says he is "already getting applications from all over the world from people who want to work there."[49]

A bit ominously, however, "About the Author" blurbs in more recent L'Amour paperbacks report that Shalako "will be a live, operating town," all right—"when it is constructed."[50]

And the final happy note. In August 1982 the Congress of the United States voted to award L'Amour a special congressional gold medal, along with similar medals to Fred Waring and to the widow of Joe Louis. L'Amour was to be honored for chronicling the settlement of the West.[51] President Ronald Reagan presented L'Amour with his medal at a White House ceremony on 24 September 1983, and called attention at that time to the recipient's "enormous contributions to Western folklore and our frontier heritage."[52] The irrepressible L'Amour is quoted as having lamented earlier the fact that Ronald Reagan never appeared in a movie based on one of his novels. "Maybe I can talk him into doing one some day," he added.[53]

Chapter Two

The Range of L'Amour's Range

Most Louis L'Amour buffs probably read their favorite Western fiction writer because of his action-stacked plots. Along the way to predictable but varied climaxes, they pause to enjoy the brilliantly painted scenery. Some savor the cinematic dialogue; fewer, perhaps, appreciate the sage advice and cautions, and the incidental history lessons. Still fewer pause over the bits of humor, if for no other reason than that they are so exceptional, so rare. Oddly, there is also relatively little violence. What there is, moreover, is controlled—explosive but brief—as in the works of Hemingway. Also, those who seek cheap sex scenes, such as disfigure the recent so-called "adult" Western, are likely to avoid L'Amour altogether.

Lots of Plots

Yes, L'Amour is best for his plots. The first technical aspect of writing that he mentioned to a recent interviewer was plotting. He remarked that he sees himself as a latter-day troubadour, a tale-teller, a campfire entertainer welcomed after the grimy work of the day is done. To audiences seeking such diversion, what happens in a story, and then what happens next—that is, plot—provides the riveting excitement. After noting that 90 percent of all fiction is based on twelve to eighteen or so basic plots, and that the Greeks, Geoffrey Chaucer, William Shakespeare, and Charles Dickens all reworked the same plot formulas, L'Amour recalled that "George[s] Polti many years ago listed 36 basic plots and nobody has ever improved on his list."[1] L'Amour is no exception to the critical truism that Western storytellers employ few of Polti's situations. Some common ones are the rivalry of a superior and an inferior, daring enterprise, a criminal pursued by an avenger, a puzzle, falling victim to cruelty, and rebellion.

Polti would have been happy to cite L'Amour's plots to illustrate, at most, armed rivalry over land, wealth, livestock; armed missions of rescue; detection; justice; and evasion, pursuit, and capture. L'Amour makes a special subgenre out of hunted turning hunter.

Frank Gruber in a classic passage in his *Pulp Jungle* reasoned that there are seven basic Western plots. They are 1) the Union Pacific Story, 2) the Ranch Story, 3) the Empire Story, 4) the Revenge Story, 5) Custer's Last Stand, 6) the Outlaw Story, and 7) the Marshal Story.[2]

L'Amour is a master at creating plots of all seven types. Thus, the early short story "Merrano and the Dry Country" (reprinted in *The Strong Shall Live*) dramatizes the triumph of a good man over prejudiced neighbors and a stubborn environment. Kilkenny, the hero of *The Mountain Valley War,* tries to homestead in Idaho but rides instead headlong into a feud between an arrogant cattle baron and family-oriented farmers. *Ride the Dark Trail* presents a feisty old widow's defense against a fat, crippled villain's nefarious scheme to rob her of her land and its fortresslike ranch. The hero of *The Burning Hills* must avenge the murder of his horse-herding partner. *Kilrone* plays variations on the Custer story by featuring an ex-army officer as hero, a military post divisively commanded, and inimical Indians also disunified. In *Son of a Wanted Man* both outlaw and foster son seek to reform, one rather late, the other in the nick of time. And the marshal in the short story "The Marshal of Sentinel" (*The Strong Shall Live*) must do more than defend his town; he must also wipe out a past mistake, aid a drunkard, and impress a woman.

L'Amour typically used Gruber's seven plots but plays variations on them. "Merrano and the Dry Side" is an early lecture on Western ecological dangers. Merrano succeeds where his neighbors fail because he cooperates with nature instead of trying to tame it: he handles water sensibly and improves vegetation. Kilkenny of *The Mountain Valley War* figures in two other Kilkenny novels. The old heroine of *Ride the Dark Trail* was a Sackett before marrying into the Talon family; hence she connects with about two dozen other L'Amour novels. *The Burning Hills* is a vengeance novel, but it also has racial elements provided by one of L'Amour's very few Hispanic heroines. Many other L'Amour novels in addition to *Kilrone* have clashes between whites and Indians; most of them, again like *Kilrone*, avoid the tiresome old Custer's Last Stand stereotypes. Often L'Amour introduces a hero whose past may be that of an outlaw but who in the present is trying so hard to mend his ways that he should be accorded the famous Western second chance. Occasionally, as in *Dark Canyon,* dirty criminal money stakes the reformed hero to such a chance. And one of the best marshal stories by

L'Amour is *Borden Chantry* (1977), which boldly introduces Borden himself even though a tenth of America read of his murder six years earlier in *North to the Rails.*

L'Amour's most common plot configuration concerns land rivalry. *Utah Blaine, Kilkenny, Guns of the Timberlands, Silver Canyon, Flint, Over on the Dry Side,* and several Sackett titles head a long list of such works. L'Amour has also written a surprising number of novels concerned with mining towns, mining, rivalry over the results, and bloody attempts to locate lost or buried treasure—including pirate gold—for example, *Taggart, Lando, The High Graders, The Empty Land, Under the Sweetwater Rim, The Ferguson Rifle,* and the recent bigger novels *Bendigo Shafter* and *Comstock Lode.* We also have some wagon-train novels, for example, *Westward the Tide* and *The Tall Stranger.* L'Amour seldom deals in a central way with gunmen, but in *The First Fast Draw* and *High Lonesome* he does, while the slight short story "One Night Stand" *(The Strong Shall Live)* spoofs the genre by showing what happens when an actor impersonates Wild Bill Hickok. A few of L'Amour's novels are about cattle drives and little else, for example, *Matagorda, Killoe,* and *Chancy.* Former detective-story writer L'Amour may be counted on to combine the who-done-it and the Western hero's story, as in *The Iron Marshal* and *Milo Talon,* and several short stories featuring L'Amour's durable hero Chick Bowdrie. *Conagher* and *The Cherokee Trail* are stage-station mini-epics, as are some early short stories, including "Alkali Basin" *(War Party)* and "Bluff Creek Station" *(The Strong Shall Live).* Several yarns defy easy pigeonholing: *Heller with a Gun,* about traveling actors and actresses in the violent West; *Sitka,* largely about Alaska; *Fair Blows the Wind,* a Raphael Sabatini-like swashbuckler; and *The Lonesome Gods,* a veritable anthology of tried-and-true L'Amour special effects, plus a few new ones.

Formula or History?

More valuable than Polti's and Gruber's separate plot categorizings is an idea by Jon Tuska. He divides Western fiction into three classes. These are the formulary narrative, the romantic historical reconstruction, and the historical reconstruction. Tuska regards the first and third groups as distinct, while the second has elements of both others.[3]

We have long loved the formulary Western and known its main ingredients. John G. Cawelti pioneered in specifying and analyzing the importance to the formula of setting, characters, and patterns of action. The setting is Western—across the Mississippi River, where distances are vast, water is scarce, and nature is hostile, where sunlight glares and darkness is intense but for diamond-clear stars, but also where nature in general—once you surrender to its conditions—can be heartstopping in its beauty.

Character patterns in formulary Western fiction are composed of combinations and permutations of the following: savages both white and otherwise, who are in the West to exploit, but also to revere and build; townspeople, including women, who seek to settle; and the lonely hero, typically a fellow with a shadowy past which need not matter now, habitually taciturn but capable of poetic utterance, adept with weapons and horses, commonly with distinctive Western garb. Women are a special subgroup. They used to be simple, pure heroines; later, heroines and "soiled doves"; still later, featured in pairs, equally good though so confusing as to cause pause in the slowly amorous hero; recently, varied and often "liberated." Savages, too, have become more skillfully characterized; hence, outlaws can reform and merit salvation; and bloodthirsty, rape-seeking redskins have been modified to include genuinely noble Indians, credibly human, hence sometimes violent but now understandably motivated—like the rest of humanity, really.[4]

Cawelti implicitly accepts the complexity of plot suggested by Polti and Gruber, but adds this valuable generalization that subsumes at least Gruber's seven types:

a kind of basic situation . . . develops out of . . . the epic moment when the values and disciplines of American society stand balanced against the savage wilderness. The situation must involve a hero who possesses some of the urges toward violence as well as the skills, heroism and personal honor ascribed to the wilderness way of life, and it must place this hero in a position where he becomes involved with or committed to the agents and values of civilization. The nature of this situation, and of the conflict between town and wilderness which lies behind it imply that the formulaic pattern of action is that of chase and pursuit because it is in this pattern that the clash of savages and townspeople manifests itself.[5]

Cawelti adds that the Western is popular because it is seen by its readers as "a brilliantly articulated game" which has opposing players, usually on two distinct sides, a set of rules permitting certain actions but not others, moving in a somewhat predictable pattern toward an anticipated end, and a "board or field" whereon such action occurs.[6] Players in this game are the characters, moves constitute plot elements, and the board may be desert, plain, forest, mountain, canyon, trail, and so on.[7]

I would add that the author of such fictions plays a game of solitaire chess, making and countering his own white and black moves, sometimes in a neat counterpoint, whereas the central character or characters on each side are playing not chess but poker. Further, when the hero bluffs, he is being heroic; but when the villain does so, he is lying.

Tuska's third category, it will be recalled, is the historical reconstruction, which is "sound historical fiction" set in the American West and written for the purpose of learning what happened in our Western past. "But the truth [Tuska adds] isn't always concerned with purely physical events; sometimes, maybe even most of the time, it has to do with spiritual events. To reclaim this past, the spiritual past, to know what happened truly and why it happened, is the primary objective. . . ."[8] Tuska is more demanding here than he was in the case of formulary Westerns, and for discussion he narrowly chooses as examples of the Western historical reconstruction Benjamin Capps's *A Woman of the People* (1966) and Matthew Braun's *Black Fox* (1972). As is not the case with formularies, the hero in the historical reconstruction is "a human being . . . while the structure is expanded to encompass . . . complexity of character and incident. . . ."[9] When we read such works "[w]e come to recognize our solidarity with people from the past; we relive their lives, face the issues which confronted them, and . . . come to some deeper understanding of ourselves. The historical reconstruction demonstrates . . . that it is possible to write fiction that is stirring and entertaining and still be historically accurate, truthful to the time, the place, and the people."[10]

In his bibliography, Tuska lists many Western historical reconstructions, by such writers as Vardis Fisher, A. B. Guthrie, Jr., Frederick Manfred, Conrad Richter, and Frank Waters. L'Amour might be outraged at being excluded, for it is his opinion that extensive historical research bulwarks much of his formulary fiction and most of his "historical" novels, and that thus he should qualify as a historical reconstructionist. But high-principled Tuska would doubtless counter that L'Amour ought to feel complimented enough to have his works placed in the degraded second category, that of romantic historical reconstructions.

This hybrid class, Tuska does grant, is illustrated by fiction with characters having more depth and powered by events having more complexity than mere formulary fiction. But he quickly adds that, in his opinion, romantic reconstructionists know little history, and not only hold that modicum in contempt but also deceitfully entertain readers by failing to appeal to their conscience.[11]

L'Amour's Formula

Why, then, is L'Amour's body of fiction so popular? After all, formulary Westerns are outmoded and romantic historical reconstructions are vapid. L'Amour is popular in spite of adverse critical opinions because he takes the two main types of Western stories—the formulary and the historical—and plays variations with them. He is also a master at giving the impression that he is sitting at a campfire with us, characterizing individual heroes and heroines and villains and many types in between, setting them into action, and above all placing them in locales that we are made to believe are real, and in times past to which we all wish we could escape for a while. L'Amour could not have succeeded if he had merely introduced changes on an utterly stale formula. Nor, evidently, does he have the patience to reconstruct history in depth, after profound research rather than his own breezy and superficial variety.

L'Amour, it must be frankly said at this point, is too popular to be defined as an absorbing critical challenge. Like E. A. Robinson and Eugene O'Neill before him, both of whom worried when they began to appeal to the masses and grow well-to-do, L'Amour ought long ago to have branched out, been innovative, taken some chances. He appears, however, to equate quality with quantity. He thinks that he ought to be a critical success because of his high sales figures. How else can one account for his saying of his 1984 block-buster novel *The Walking Drum* that he wrote it "15 years ago but my publisher got me to put it on the shelf. He didn't know what a favor he was doing me. . . . Because now it's worth a good deal more money than it was then."[12]

Why, instead, did L'Amour not insist that Bantam in 1970 ballyhoo the new L'Amour, the emerging romanticist of the medieval Middle East? Because sales figures might slump. I wish that he had back then taken a leaf from Herman Melville, who hated himself for following his critically challenging but unpopular *Mardi* with two lesser books, *Redburn* and *White-Jacket,* and accordingly griped about them to his father-in-law: "my only desire for their 'success' (as it is called) springs from my pocket, & not my heart. So far as I am individually concerned,

& independent of my pocket, it is my earnest desire to write those sort of books which are said to 'fail.'—pardon this egotism."[13] Melville's royalties suffered, to be sure. But, unlike too many youthful American literary winners, he varied his early patterns and achieved artistic grandeur.

Place and Time

Two of L'Amour's most enduring attributes are his impressionistic evocation of faraway places and his compelling reconstructions of long-ago times. A pleasant way to suggest his sweep is to indicate the spread of his works through time, mainly in the nineteenth century, but into other centuries in a few novels as well, and also to note a geographical spread reaching over continents and showing no signs of letting up.

The earliest action in any L'Amour novel to date is that of a humble coyote back in seventh-century Utah, or what was to become Utah. L'Amour begins *The Empty Land* with a mini-lecture on history: about Pope Gregory the Great, the Golden Age of scholarship in Ireland, the Merovingian kings on the Continent, the war between Champa ("now called South Vietnam") and China, about T'ang in China, and also "a relatively unknown young man named Mohammed . . . in Mecca" (p. 1). More importantly for American civilization, L'Amour's seventh-century coyote dug into a chipmunk hole, failed to find its meal, but enlarged the opening for water and a juniper root, which was nourished and grew, and in time exposed gold—for a trapper to find in 1824. (Then the main events of the story transpire in 1848.)

Now 1824 is early for L'Amour but not by any means his earliest narrative date. *The Walking Drum* takes us back to late twelfth-century Europe and the Middle East. Reminiscences in *Fair Blows the Wind* go back to 1577, and most of the action involving progenitor Tatton Chantry occurs shortly before 1588, the year of the disastrous Spanish Armada. The earliest action in any Sackett novel occurs in 1599, when in *Sackett's Land* the young hero Barnabas Sackett leaves the well-depicted fens of Wales first for Elizabethan London and then the sparse Carolinas. *To the Far Blue Mountains* and *The Warrior's Path* take up subsequent action, on to 1630. L'Amour explains that Barnabas's New World home in Shooting Creek may be located now off the highway between Franklin, North Carolina, and Chattanooga, Tennessee, while his death site is in the mountains above Crab Orchard.[14] The Talon saga starts with Jean Talon leaving the rugged Gaspé Peninsula in

northeastern Canada in 1821, for fame, fortune, and romance south
and then far west—all in *Rivers West.*

These Chantry, Sackett, and Talon family sagas pose vexing time
problems, some segments having contradictory evidence, others insuf-
ficient evidence. They all start early; yet if L'Amour fulfills his grand
promises he will carry the histories of these exciting families back into
still earlier epochs and also forward into the twentieth century.

The action in all but one of the other novels is in the nineteenth
century, and with few exceptions in the 1860s, 1870s, and 1880s.
Major events in one Chantry novel, *The Ferguson Rifle,* take place about
1804, although it starts in rural North Carolina in 1780. Action in
another Chantry story, *North to the Rails,* may transpire as late as 1890,
during a cattle drive north of Santa Fe; but this dating may be the
consequence of carelessness on L'Amour's part. Only Sackett activities—not those of Chantrys or Talons—to date occur in the 1810s,
1820s, and 1830s. *The Tall Stranger,* the beginning of *Sitka, Down the
Long Hills,* most of *The Empty Land, The Californios,* and *Ride the River*
detail events cast in the 1840s. Actions in *Killoe, The Quick and the
Dead,* and most of *The Lonesome Gods* may be dated in the 1850s.
L'Amour seems not eager to detail much Western action immediately
before the Civil War.

Nor has L'Amour to date cast much fiction in the tragic Civil War
years, perhaps through fear of losing Southern readers because of his
pro-Union sentiments. Most of his dozen or so 1860s novels start after
the war. True, *The Cherokee Trail* takes place mostly in 1864, but the
central character is the widow of a Civil War officer and has gone west
to run a rugged Colorado stagecoach station. The hero of *Under the
Sweetwater Rim,* which also details events during 1864, is an army officer on leave who discomfits a villain seeking to supply rifles to Indians between Fort Laramie and Fort Bridger. L'Amour dates many of
his 1860s novels by alluding to the Civil War as recently ended, for
example, in *Conagher, Callaghen,* and *The Iron Marshal.* In doing so
here, as sometimes elsewhere, he is precise as to the date. Thus, *The
Shadow Riders* begins exactly at the end of the war and carries us down
into southeastern Texas, by the Gulf of Mexico. Action in *The Man
from Skibbereen,* placed in Wyoming territory, is dated October 1868.
And so on.

Action in fully a third of L'Amour's novels occurs in the dramatic
1870s. Thus, *Lonely on the Mountain,* since it features a cameo appearance by Louis Riel between the time of his rebellion in northwestern

Canada and his escape from its consequences, must transpire in the summer of 1870. L'Amour dates *Chancy* 1871. We read in *Brionne* that U.S. Grant is campaigning for reelection; hence the main action of the novel comes in 1872. Sometimes L'Amour remains more general. In *Mojave Crossing* we are told that the famous outlaw Tiburcio Vásquez (1835–75) was captured only recently, in the area of tiny Los Angeles. In *Crossfire Trail* we merely read that General George Armstrong Custer is now in the Badlands, northeast of the fictive action. *Kilkenny* events occur after the death of Wild Bill Hickok (1837–76). In both *The Key-Lock Man* and *Son of a Wanted Man* mention is made of Jesse James's disastrous raid (in September 1876) on Northfield, Minnesota. Occasionally L'Amour flat out gives us a precise date, as in *The Sackett Brand,* in which narrator Tell Sackett, after burying his murdered wife, dates her grave cross 25 April 1877. Sometimes L'Amour prefers to be coy. For example, we read in *The Rider of Lost Creek* that the villain down in Texas has a Winchester '73, and the hero remarks that the fact is unusual.

Novels detailing events in the 1880s are fewer in number than those concerned with the 1870s. *Taggart* is set in 1880; *Shalako,* in the spring of 1882. But the other half dozen or so are datable only more loosely. Thus, we can pin down the time of action in *The Mountain Valley War* in southwestern Idaho territory only as between the death of Johnny Ringo (1844?–82) and the 1890 admission of Idaho as a state.

Some but not many of L'Amour's novels narrate fiction and historical events spreading out over years, even decades. Thus, *Sitka* starts about 1845 in central Pennsylvania, carries its hero to sea and even to Russia, and continues to the time of the Alaska Purchase in 1867. *Reilly's Luck* ends about 1882, since it is said that the new town of Durango is now about two years old; the story starts in wintry Montana about 1861 (although no mention is made of the Civil War) with the hero a mere child of four, destined for picaresque episodes as far away as Europe. *Bendigo Shafter* opens in 1859 and moves through to the time of the enfranchisement of women in Wyoming in 1870. *Comstock Lode* begins in remote Cornwall in 1849, with the future hero a youngster, whom the complex story will take to young adulthood in 1859, 1860, and finally 1861—with news of the Civil War reaching him in western Nevada; bustling San Francisco is also vividly evoked.

The action of a few L'Amour novels cannot be dated, even within a decade or so. Obviously these cowboy and frontier books dramatize

events of the 1870s or thereabouts. Examples include *Utah Blaine,
Guns of the Timberlands* (which has an ex-Texas Ranger for hero), *The
Burning Hills,* and *Fallon.*

Charmingly, L'Amour carries the action of a couple of fictional
pieces beyond the climax by means of thumbnail sketches of descendants of main characters. Thus, at the end of *Dark Canyon* we read of
a certain great-grandson killed during the Korean War. The hero of
The High Graders is disappointed when his grandson "became an ad
man on Madison Avenue" (p. 166). So too in the short story "Bluff
Creek Station" (*The Strong Shall Live*), at the end of which we read that
a motel has now replaced the old stage station, but also that descendants of the hero died in the Argonne Forest, Normandy, and Vietnam.

Many of L'Amour's non-Western short stories are set in the twentieth century, but thus far only one novel is. That is *The Broken Gun,*
which is really a Western that wandered beyond its proper time and
that is narrated by and stars as hero an autobiographical character—
200 pounds in weight, combat veteran (of the Korean and Vietnamese
Wars), ex-boxer, successful writer and researcher, man of action in the
West (here, Arizona) in 1962 or so. When asked about the new frontier
(space), twentieth-century technological cowboys (astronauts), and
their latter-day steeds (space capsules), L'Amour replied without a trace
of shyness that he has written no space fiction yet, but he added, "I
may. I've often thought about it. I certainly will do some writing on
the subject."[15] So, just as he is now turning back to the twelfth-century
Middle East, he may also be turning forward and upward to twenty-
first-century Mars, and beyond. With L'Amour, the sky is not the
limit.

Short-Fiction Time and Place

The action in most of L'Amour's reprinted Western short stories is,
like that of his novels, generally to be dated 1850–80. The collections
are *War Party, The Strong Shall Live, Buckskin Run, Bowdrie, Law of the
Desert Born,* and *Bowdrie's Law.* Some of the tales therein are rehearsals
for later novels. "Trap of Gold" (*War Party, Law of the Desert Born*)
became part of *Taggart;* "War Party" (*War Party*), part of *Bendigo Shafter;* "Booty for a Badman" (*War Party*) introduced happy readers to our
favorite Sackett, Tell Sackett; "The Gift of Cochise" (*War Party*), itself
prepared for by "Ride, You Tonto Raiders!" (*Law of the Desert Born*),
led to *Hondo* (as mentioned) and overtured L'Amour's spectacular suc-

cess. Curiously, "Ride, You Tonto Raiders!," a 1949 story that L'Amour failed to recopyright and that hence found its way into Carrol & Graf's mischievous duty-free collection, introduced a half-dozen or more themes developed in better, later L'Amour works. "Hattan's Castle" (*The Strong Shall Live*) is a partial preview of *The Empty Land.*

The eight short stories reprinted in *Bowdrie* and the ten in *Bowdrie's Law* may be loosely dated as to action in the late 1870s and early 1880s. They feature Texas Ranger Chick Bowdrie, who ranges throughout the Southwest like a celebate knight of old. Two other collections of short fiction, *Yondering* and *The Hills of Homicide,* are cast in the twentieth century and are, to speak with charity, hardly vintage L'Amour. Neither collection would have sold out a first printing if issued under either of L'Amour's erstwhile pen names. *Yondering* features mostly sea adventures in Far Eastern waters, probably in the 1920s and 1930s, and seems partly autobiographical. Thrown in for good measure are a couple of so-so war tales, one concerning the Spanish Foreign Legion in the 1920s, another, freedom fighters against the Nazis in Greece in 1941. *The Hills of Homicide* presents eight Dashiell Hammett-like hard-boiled detective stories originally published in 1947–52 pulps and sketching contemporary seamy life. Only the title story, cast in and near Las Vegas, and also a piece entitled "Stay Out of My Nightmare," played out in Los Angeles, are worth more than a passing glance. Both are redolent of old black-and-white George Raft and Humphrey Bogart flicks, and in their era might have done well if adapted for the screen.

Chapter Three
L'Amour at Dawn

The *New Western Magazine* of 6 August 1949 featured a short story entitled "Ride, You Tonto Raiders!" by L'Amour. It is a near-microcosm of the fictional world that he subsequently created. The story dropped from sight until Carroll & Graf noted that it was in the public domain and included it in their publication of several such Western yarns by L'Amour, who immediately ordered Bantam to rush *Law of the Desert Born* into print to meet the competition. Bantam's collection also includes "Ride, You Tonto Raiders!"

Ingredients for Success

The story stars Mathurin "Matt" Sabre. (Any relation to Sam Spade or Mike Hammer?) Matt is a former buffalo hunter, prospector in Mexico, revolutionist in Central America, foreign legionnaire in Morocco, vacationer in France and elsewhere, Texas trail herder, marshal of Mobeetie, Texas. Tall, broad-shouldered, lightning-quick, he wounds Billy Curtin in an El Paso gunfight, and dying Billy begs him to deliver some $5,000 to his widow, Jenny, ranching with their son Billy, Jr., in the Tonto Basin outside Yellowjacket, Arizona. Doing so, Matt discovers that Prince McCarran covets Jenny's land, and also that he is aided by saloon- and mine-owner Galusha Reed, fast-gun Tony Sikes, and bumbling town marshal Sid Trumbull. The hero quickly likes Jenny a lot, is reluctant to explain how her husband died, but wants to save her land. He is befriended by the following: Simpson, a canny codger; stableman Camp Gordon, who was Cambridge educated, drinks too much, and spouts Shakespeare; Keys, a saloon piano-player who once knew Johann Strauss, Jr., in Vienna; old Tom Judson and half-breed Silerado "Rado," both of whom work loyally for Jenny; and Pepito Fernandez, grandson of the Hispanic from whom Curtin legitimately purchased his land.

More important than the story, however, are two other elements. They are character bromides and stylistic features. We have here half the stereotypical relationships and actions of L'Amour's future fiction. Matt's military and cosmopolitan background previews that of many later L'Amour heroes, for example, those featured in *Showdown at Yellow Butte, Kilrone, Crossfire Trail,* and *Shalako.* Killing the man whose wife the hero will later marry prefigures the situation in *Hondo,* as does the fact that the heroine—red-headed, as are a third of L'Amour's most fetching females—has a son for whom the hero becomes surrogate father. Such fathers are so frequent in L'Amour that one wonders whether he is trying to point an autobiographical moral. In *To Tame a Land* the hero shatters the pattern by oedipally killing his surrogate father. In *Milo Talon* the heroine has a surrogate father, while in *The Cherokee Trail* and *The Lonesome Gods* the heroines play the role of surrogate mother.

The ineptness of the marshal in "Ride, You Tonto Raiders!" means that the hero must take the law into his own hands, as is frequent in L'Amour. In addition, when Rafe Collins, an honest lawman up from El Paso, confronts Matt and offers to arrest him, Matt so impresses the man with his solidity and courtesy that Rafe backs off. This is reminiscent of several later fictional works, notably *The Proving Trail.* The hero's hiring of Pepito anticipates L'Amour's admirable absence of racial prejudice. L'Amour once remarked that there are no "ethnic villains" in his fiction,[1] forgetting Chico Cruz of *The Daybreakers.* Eddie Holt of *Hanging Woman Creek* is L'Amour's most memorable black to date. The ultimate in heroic color blindness comes when Tatton Chantry of *Fair Blows the Wind* marries an Inca-Peruvian.

One oddly stressed characteristic of early L'Amour heroes, fortuitously absent in his later fiction, is their berserker fighting lust. It appears repeatedly in Matt in "Ride, You Tonto Raiders!," and subsequently in Utah Blaine and Kilkenny (in *Kilkenny* but not in *The Mountain Valley War*), Clay Bell (*Guns of the Timberlands*), and Trace Jordan (*The Burning Hills*), among others, but not, blessedly, in Matt Brennan (*Silver Canyon*) or Matt Coburn (*The Empty Land*).

Gothic fiction as they are, Western novels often feature lots of hidden documents. "Ride, You Tonto Raiders!" is no exception. After the final fight, during which the villain suffers a broken nose—a tedious feature in ex-pugilist L'Amour's stories—Matt finds documents to validate Jenny's claim to the land. Other L'Amour fiction uses this paper chestnut far too frequently. For the best example, see *The Broken Gun,* which starts with a document stuffed in a gun barrel and ends with the digging out of another document. An odd use of the printed page

and also the written-on page comes in *Over on the Dry Side,* in which a
Tennyson poem offers a clue to the location of a handwritten document
of great historical value.

As for stylistic features—the hero of "Ride, You Tonto Raiders!" uses
eyes, patience, thought-filled silence, and instinct compelling him to
berserker action—against villains thoughtfully timing their one-on-
one confrontations with said hero—to the goal of peace at the hearth.
Key words in L'Amour's writings—all used repeatedly in "Ride, You
Tonto Raiders!"—include "alone," "eye," "home," "intuition," "patience," "shoulder," "silence," "violence," and especially "trouble"
(used eighteen times here). We also have typical L'Amour nonforeshadowing. For example, the hero promises to drift on but then does not
keep that reader-teasin' promise. It is well to have the hero named
quickly. But here as elsewhere L'Amour throws too many other names
at us too fast: in less than a full page are named six townspeople important in subsequent action, with the name of one of them not mentioned again for more than twenty pages. Place names, too, bombard
us with little let-up: in one paragraph we are asked to follow the hero
up Shirt Tail Creek, across Bloody Basin and Skeleton Ridge to the
Verde River, near which is Hardscrabble Creek. L'Amour is partly
characteristic here in dating his action only by indirections: Matt once
ordered Wes Hardin (who flourished with guns circa 1871–78) out of
Mobeetie; further, Major Randall surprised some Apaches, we read,
near Turret Butte "only a few years before" (p. 124), that is, in March
1873. L'Amour paces his action by alternating close-up scenes (with
credible dialogue) and panoramic summary—and all with habitual
changes in narrative point of view.

Stylistic infelicities have endemically marred L'Amour's prose for
decades. Notable in this 1949 story are his use of pronouns without
proper antecedents, "due to" as adverb, "less" for "fewer," "only" out
of place, parallelism violated, awkward "That"-clauses as sentence
openers, "There's two," and clichés.

On to *Hondo*

Now to proceed through L'Amour's numerous novels, touching on
each but concentrating only on the best, to show such versatility as is
manifest by stressing new elements as the years and decades pass:

Westward the Tide is L'Amour's first novel.[2] It was published in England in 1950, and was not available in the United States until Bantam

reissued it in 1977. It is rousing and suspenseful. Its hero is Mathieu "Matt" Bardoul, former Army officer and survivor of the August 1867 Wagon Box Fight. It is now 1877, Custer is dead, and a wagon train of generally inept families is heading past Deadwood for Black Hills gold. Matt joins the train mainly because he likes wagoneer Brian Coyle and his peppy but naive daughter Jacquine. A tangle of villains, led by Clive Massey and supported by cowardly ex-army officer Orvis Pearson (under whom Matt served down in Apacheria), plans to join the wagoneers to massacre and pillage, then to seek Black Hills gold at their ease. Suspense is provided by the reluctance of most good people in the wagon train to trust Matt, who is badmouthed by both Massey and Pearson. Subplots galore: a fellow shadows the train with a wagon of his own and a wanted person of one sex or the other in it, a member of the good faction is along for the purpose of locating his brother's murderer, etc.

Historical background is excellently sketched in *Westward the Tide.* We see the real Deadwood, attend real-life Jack Langrishe's dramatic show at his Gem Theatre there, and even bump into Calamity Jane.[3] Portugee Phillips, real-life Western hero of the 230-mile horseback ride from Fort Phil Kearny to Fort Laramie in the $-50°$ dead of winter after the December 1866 Fetterman Massacre, gives Jacquine a favorable character reference concerning his good friend Matt. Not content to let history glint obliquely, L'Amour pauses here and there to present direct lectures on Custer, Black Hills gold, the Sioux, the consequences of Custer's death, Indian statesmanship and reverence for the land, mountain men's lives, the buffalo, European economic hardship vs. the American pioneering spirit, and real-life Western gunmen. Also present are two gratuitous cracks concerning higher education and teachers. The hero says, "it seems to me the advantage of academic education is somewhat overrated"; later he quietly thinks that weak Colonel Pearson should have avoided a military career and instead "should have been teaching in a grade school or the floor walker in a department store" (pp. 28, 214).

Oh, the hero is macho enough, here as elsewhere in L'Amour's works. Matt is shot in the shoulder, later shot in the side and head (he removes the bullet from his own skull), still later stabbed by an Indian. As is frequent in L'Amour, the hero, when wounded at one point, is separated from succor and wanders horseless over hostile terrain. L'Amour escalates violence in which the hero is involved. In chapter 3, he slaps a would-be assailant and dunks him in a horse trough. In

chapter 9 he fistfights another adversary and—predictably—breaks his
nose. Last, in chapter 12 Matt taunts the main villain into a gunfight.
All wandering, punching, and shooting consummated, hero and heroine are free to make a home together, with a hearthfire. Embracing
Jacquine, Matt predicts that she will become a good ranch wife and
puts in his order for fifteen children.

Westward the Tide is unusual for being diagrammably structured into
neat quarters of three chapters each; but it seems weak through having
a few plot hints—stolen ammunition, tell-tale scars—not followed up.
And why so very many characters whose names begin with the letter
"B"? We have Bain, Ban, Bardoul, Barney, Batsell, Ben Hardy, Ben
Speery, Bill, Boyne, Braden, Brian, Brooks, Buckskin, Buffalo, and
Bunker.

Next was *Showdown at Yellow Butte* (1953), which despite its popu-
larity is hasty and weak, by comparison to most of L'Amour's later
works. In his introduction to the 1980 Gregg Press reprint, Scott R.
McMillan tries to show that it goes beyond the formula, avoids the
faults of the amoral "adult" Western of today, and is both romantic as
to faith in the West and realistic in its use of detail. McMillan also
praises the minor characters in this work, the hero of which brings a
past of varied experience to bear in the fight against greedy Easterners
who would dispossess hard-working, land-respecting ranchers. Notable are Mrs. Taggart, who shotguns her husband's killer, and Connie
Duane, a woman from the East, whom the West must reform quickly.
This is L'Amour's first range-war novel and is followed by a score or so
of the same sort but with more artistry.

Hondo (1953) is a remarkable early novel.[4] It has a classically simple
plot. Hondo Lane is a scout and dispatch rider for General George
Crook in Arizona in 1874. Hondo aids a ranch woman named Angie
Lowe and her six-year-old son, Johnny, who are periodically deserted
by their no-good husband and father Ed, whom Hondo later saves but
still later kills when the foolish man turns murderous. Hondo is captured by Apaches under Vittoro, is tortured but then saved because
Angie lies that he is her missing husband. Hondo duels with Silva, a
vicious Apache rival for Angie's hand. In the background is the United
States Army, that symbol of relentlessly advancing white "civilization." Probably few today read *Hondo* without picturing John Wayne
as its titular hero.

Michael T. Marsden rightly notes that *Hondo* follows the "culturally
determined pattern" of "formula fiction" but rises above the formulary

"by contributing innovative elements to an always changing and evolv-
ing story form."[5] Marsden then notes that Hondo mediates between
the progressive white world and Apacheria, epitomized by Vittoro the
aging chief. I should add that L'Amour himself similarly mediates between both twentieth-century Western wildness and the conservative
American fictional form, on the one hand, and twentieth-century readers, largely urban, on the other. Marsden opines that Ed Lowe is
doomed because he is a hindrance to white civilization. Here I would
argue that Hondo is no more civilized than Vittoro—or Silva either. I
would say, with Francis Parkman, who epically narrated the clash of
two ways of life in New-World nature, that the tragedy once again is
not that one human side lost but that nature lost. Surely Apacheria has
been conquered far less than it has been simply ruined. Marsden is on
safer ground when he reasons that Hondo is the ranging male principle
and Angie the ranching, domestic female principle, and that the
"omega point," their final staying point, "is clearly hearth and home,
the end of all westward movement."[6]

We have cosmic balances in *Hondo*. The army is bungling but contains some brave men. The Apaches number in their midst fine Vittoro
and mean Silva. Hondo tells his new white woman about his former
redskin squaw Destarte ("Morning"). He also explains to Angie that
Apaches never lie and that an Apache couple in love simply tell each
other "verlebena" ("forever"). (Yet they practiced polygamy and beat
their wives.) Curiously, Angie quite properly saves Hondo by a flat lie;
further, he lies to her when he says that her husband died bravely.
Hondo undertakes to educate Johnny by letting the dog Sam snap at
the boy and by taking him to "school" in the Apache-infested desert,
which is murderously arid and yet occasionally experiences rain in tor-
rents. Action is thunderous here; yet the word "silence" is employed
at least two dozen times.[7]

More Formularies

Utah Blaine (1954), though immensely popular, represents a typical
retrogression on L'Amour's part. It is standard formulary fiction at its
goriest. Wayne C. Lee can praise it only for its smoothly managed plot,
its big, fast, smart hero, the shadings of characterization of its villains,
and its well-painted sets.[8] Utah Blaine rescues an innocent old man
who is being lynched by land-greedy villains, inherits a ranch from the
grateful man when he is murdered later, fights to preserve that new

turf by outsmarting all thugs, chooses a brave female homesteader (named Angie again) rather than a murdered neighbor's spoiled daughter, regenerates a would-be ruffian by the violence of beating his face half off and then offering him a job, and is aided by a canny newspaperman. We can detect a score of Western stereotypes in the novel. At the same time, it is embarrassingly readable, rollicking in its healthy outdoor mayhem, and satisfying in the way it deals out rewards at the end, in the good old-fashioned Hollywood way. It is noteworthy that its hero is, I believe, the first in L'Amour of a crowded sequence of tough men consciously aware of their own body odor. Perhaps gamey Utah wants wife, home, and well water so that he will be tempted to bathe more often.

In 1954 L'Amour published *Kilkenny*. Although in its story line it is the last of a trilogy concerning a Shane-like legendary gunman helper of others, it was the first to be published. The other two are *The Rider of Lost Creek* (1976) and *The Mountain Valley War* (1978). L'Amour has explained that these three novels "were published in such a way that the first *book* to appear was the last one to be written, and the first and second books were published later. It is confusing [he rightly adds] but things sometimes happen that way."[9] Fawcett published *Kilkenny*, but Bantam issued the other two Kilkenny novels. The hero (with pseudonyms Lance and Trent) is such a loner that as L'Amour moves him from episode to episode only two friends link the action. They are gorgeous Nita Riordan and her half-breed bodyguard Jaime Brigo. (*Kilkenny* is the earliest L'Amour novel in which the hero does not marry the heroine by book's end.)

Though popular, these Kilkenny books do not show L'Amour varying much from his pattern of formulary fiction. In them the hero is more adept with guns and fists than Bardoul or Hondo are. In *Kilkenny* are some nineteen killings. The story features a foolish lawman, by now a common ingredient. At the end of *The Rider of Lost Creek* the hero, wounded four times but nursed back to legendary fitness by Nita, avoids marriage because he must quest on. Such an open ending is inevitable, given L'Amour's desire to have the fellow become an almost mythic helper figure in the West. By the time of *The Mountain Valley War*, Kilkenny is also a patriarchal figure, though still young: at one point he arms a foster son by ceremonially presenting him a Sharps rifle; at another, he gives away the lad's sister to a deserving neighbor man. By this time L'Amour was evidently surrendering to late-1970s taste: he places much of the violence offstage, including an ambush, a suicide, and the wrecking of the villain's saloon by out-of-town miners.

The hero of *Crossfire Trail* (1954) is the first of several ex-sailor cowboys created by L'Amour. There will be fine ones later, but none more courageous and internationally versatile than Rafe Caradec here. His background owes something to the author's own seafaring youth. As Keith Jarrod has observed, Rafe is a hero of mythic dimensions.[10] While at sea, he promised a dying shipmate that he would eventually get to Painted Rock, Wyoming, and save the family ranch for the man's widow and daughter. He commits justifiable mutiny to begin honoring his pledge, picks up trusted cronies across land from California's golden shore, persuades the doubtful heroine of his honesty, and defends himself against a myriad of foes—the heroine's villainous fiancé, corrupt town officials, and even a few Sioux whose ire is being aroused by Custer in their Badlands. Rafe is handy not only with his guns but also with his courtroom tongue.

A Long Plateau

By the mid-1950s L'Amour seems to have hit a plateau. His next five novels are undistinguished and do not offer appreciably new features to the old formula.

Heller with a Gun (1955) inspired a dramaturgically authentic movie (*Heller in Pink Tights*) but is a weak novel. It is important in the evolution of L'Amour as frontier writer only because in it he first presents actors and actresses traveling and performing through the West. Later he will characterize Western thespians in such better works as *Reilly's Luck* and *Comstock Lode*. The hero of the mistitled *Heller with a Gun* is like that of the earlier *Showdown at Yellow Butte:* here King Mabry also declines an unsavory job, switches sides, and is therefore hunted by his replacement. And here, as in *Utah Blaine,* we have two good women, the better of whom the hero chooses in the end. Teen-aged Dodie Saxon, a sexy, West-toughened dancer, bides her time until old Janice Ryan, from Virginia, foolishly dumps Mabry because she cannot stomach the violence he employs to save her life. In an echo from Zane Grey's *Riders of the Purple Sage,* Janice even demands that Mabry hang up his guns—or no kiss, sir—which like Grey's Lassiter he fortunately declines to do. Janice is better off with Tom Bealy, the decent manager of the inept troupe. Geographical movement here is steadily west from Nebraska territory though wintry Cheyenne to Ernest Haycox's Alder

Gulch and Virginia City. Only the first half of *Heller with a Gun* is well plotted and has good dialogue.

Rye Taylor, the hero of *To Tame a Land* (1955), loses his father when the two are abandoned while wagoning west and are attacked by Indians. The lad is then aided by Logan Pollard, who as surrogate father teaches him violence all too well but also to read. To read what? Plutarch, no less. Rye's picaresque growing-up years are detailed too hastily: then rather too quickly he becomes a plutocratic cattleman. Unexciting love for a girl and an exciting sequence of some ten killings by Rye culminate in his even shooting Pollard, who under another name has become Rye's rival for the girl's hand. (L'Amour will touch glancingly on this same unpleasant father-son sexual rivalry in *Lando*.) *To Tame a Land* is hideously violent, well paced through changes of locale, notable for the fine friendships which Rye enjoys; but it is marred by demeaning portrayals of women and by Rye's inexplicable decision to settle in Virginia. And must an orphan kill his surrogate father? And why should Rye read Plutarch and then behave as he does?

Guns of the Timberlands (1955) builds yet another ingenious plot but has value in L'Amour's development only through its well-dramatized rivalry between the hero, who wishes to preserve good land for graze through scientific handling of adjacent timber, and the villain, who does not mind upsetting the ecological balance by logging off the trees for quick profit. The most significant line in the whole novel, a line often reasserted later by L'Amour, is voiced by an old pioneer: "Two kinds of men here [in the West]. . . . Them that come to build, and them that come to get rich and get out" (p. 14). The Eastern-miseducated heroine, whom L'Amour engages to the villain to delay more heroic romancing, is reprogrammed by Western forces in due time. The cast of characters is too extensive for L'Amour to handle through direct action; accordingly, some merely drop out or obediently leave when ordered out.

The Burning Hills (1956) is a simple revenge yarn. Trace Jordan, the hero, must take the law violently into his own hands when the evil son of a powerful rancher kills Trace's partner. A new element is Hispanic heroine Maria Cristina Chavero, who provides credible love interest but also, through prejudice against gringos, less credible suspense. This short, five-chapter novel gains in complexity through L'Amour's cleverly starting it in medias res, then backing up the action by a flashback to explain why Trace is now being relentlessly pursued by trackers across the burning lava of Texas Flat.

Silver Canyon (1956) is a mish-mash of L'Amour's best effects and as such was a perfect choice as the start-up volume of Bantam's 1980 hardcover Louis L'Amour Collection. It has everything: hero strong but tired of wandering, reluctant heroine (hero promises marriage at first sight and suggests six sons), heroine's father in midst of range war, villain with murderous past in army and an eye on heroine, good old rancher who wills his spread to helpful hero and then is killed off, spineless old sheriff, crooked lawyer in nearby town, evidence planted against hero, silver lode waiting to be unearthed, and skillful vectoring of enemy plot lines. All thrilling. But almost nothing new here except the combination, which—to be sure—is improved by unusually skillful scenic description, good dialogue, and occasional poetic prose.

Two Hits and a Miss

With *Last Stand at Papago Wells* L'Amour made a splendid step forward again. Then followed *The Tall Stranger,* which is weak. Next came *Sitka,* one of his best. All three appeared in 1957.

Last Stand at Papago Wells is a beautifully constructed narrative about ten units of people, alone or in small groups, converging on an Arizona desert hellhole called Papago Wells. Hero Logan Cates is heading west to it. An eloping couple, Grant Kimbrough and Jennifer Fair, stop there on their intended way to Yuma. Her tough father Jim Fair and his men pursue the pair to Papago Wells. A lone survivor of a white party butchered by Apaches escapes to it. A teen-aged girl named Junie escapes to it by waiting until her six rape-inclined Indian captors pause to gorge themselves on mule meat; then they follow her. Churupati and his twenty-one rogue Apache-Yaquis approach the Wells in search of spoils, then circle it to attack. An old buffalo hunter named Jim Beaupre and an anti-Apache Pima named Tony Lugo, who have been forced earlier into deadly gunplay in Yuma, now escape to the Wells. The military remnants of a rag-tag posse pursues Beaupre and Lugo (and en route aid Junie) to Papago Wells. And Big Maria gallops in from Tucson laden with suspiciously heavy saddlebags.

All of this in the first six chapters. In the last ten the Apaches close in, while the little crowd in their sandy sanctuary argue about leadership, strategy, desertion, counterattacking, and whether Big Maria has gold in those saddlebags. Punctuating this suspenseful tale of a ship-like oasis of desert fools and wise ones, all pressed by Churupati, whom we never lay eyes on, is death after death—a dozen in all and in varied

ways. As Samuel Johnson said of *Paradise Lost,* no one would wish this
literary work to be any longer; but L'Amour's sense of pace here is
exhilarating, and his story flashes with excellent bits.[11]

The Tall Stranger is another wagons-west novel. It repeats some of
the cliché actions from *Westward the Tide,* starts in medias res and then
turns back (as in *The Burning Hills*) to explain why the hero, who saves
some wagon people, is mistrusted, and is altogether the weakest L'A-
mour novel to its date. Characters are introduced badly, then are
stacked offstage for later use; only villainous types die of their wounds,
while several good men survive theirs; and the romance elements are
hackneyed.

Then, as with *Last Stand at Papago Wells,* L'Amour stepped partly
out of the morass of formulary fiction, this time with his first grand
romantic historical reconstruction, *Sitka.* Its donnée is the intrigue
surrounding the Alaska Purchase. At 245 pages in paperback, *Sitka* is
half again as long as the average of his first thirteen novels. It is epic
by comparison, sweeping, too, with a bold new look. It exemplifies
L'Amour's most extensive use thus far of history, which appears here
not only in the background but at times in the foreground too, since
the hero, Jean LaBarge, is a friend from childhood of real-life Robert
J. Walker (1801–69), Pennsylvania lawyer, United States senator from
Mississippi, United States Secretary of the Treasury (1845–49), and
federal financial wizard—but "forgotten [L'Amour laments here] in the
march of history" (p. 223). Rob Walker was active behind the scenes
with Secretary of State William H. Seward, Senators Charles Sumner,
William P. Fessenden, and William H. Stewart, and Russian Ambas-
sador Edouard de Stoeckl—to all of whom and more Jean LaBarge
dances fictional attendance in various ways.

Jean LaBarge was L'Amour's most complete hero before Mathurin
Kerbouchard of *The Walking Drum.* As a youngster along the Susquehanna River, LaBarge traps and forages without parents, since his
mother is dead and his father, Smoke LaBarge, has drifted west to
become a mountain man. Jean follows in time, gets to Independence,
Missouri, then far beyond, to become seasoned by a variety of experiences: he traps, reads Plutarch, Homer, and the Bible, lives briefly
with Ute Indians as their captive, hears about Alaska from famed Pierre
Choteau in St. Louis, and is shanghaied to China. Behold the hero
now, at age twenty-one: "Jean LaBarge looked what he was, a man
born to the wild places and the tall winds. The mountain years had

shaped him for strength and molded him for trial, the desert had dried him out and the sea had made him thoughtful. His boyhood in the Great Swamp near the Susquehanna had given promise of the man he had become" (p. 41). Next LaBarge gets his own schooner (which he renames the *Susquehanna*) out of San Francisco and illegally delivers wheat to hungry Sitka, Alaska, thus tangling with cruel Russians, both those in office and those involved in commercial crime.

How can L'Amour present this swashbuckling cosmopolitan specimen of masculinity in adventurous episodes and yet include a love interest which will not tease him into settling too quickly for hearthfire, home, and children? The author brilliantly makes Jean fall in love with a glorious Russian beauty named Princess Helena de Gagarin, now the wife of decent, lovable old Russian Count Alexander Rotcheff, thirty years their elder. This diplomat, now in San Francisco, is also the bitter enemy of Baron Paul Zinnovy, the corrupt, depraved power-thirsty villain of *Sitka*.

This novel is the best structured of any thus far by L'Amour. Its thirty-six short chapters fall into nine unnumbered parts, including three intercalary units of one chapter each (chapters 5, 21, and 33). First we see Jean as a Pennsylvania lad; then he goes west and matures; next he meets Helena, Rotcheff, and Zinnovy, and gets his schooner. In the middle third Jean eludes his enemies and delivers his cargo to Sitka, buys furs, and makes a gigantic profit; a year passes, loves remain platonic but warm, villain wounds old husband, and hero and heroine must escape together, to—of all places—St. Petersburg, which is rendered with much verisimilitude. The last third includes too much: an affray between LaBarge and a professional Russian duelist, which is breathtakingly modulated, and the hero's audience with Helena's uncle, Czar Alexander II; the hero's return to Washington, D.C., to lobby for Alaska, but then an almost comic-book sequence of rushed panels—Jean's ship destroyed, Jean sent to Siberia but returned to Sitka as a convict laborer (through Stoeckl's good offices), and then—but why reveal the operatic finale?[12]

Sitka has well-oiled plot pivots. For example, Jean sells wheat in Alaska just as Count Rotcheff and his party happen to be making their way there. Consequences when Zinnovy shoots the old count flow naturally. The overland portage of Jean's lean schooner is an epic cliffhanger. But the novel has weaknesses too. Why does Zinnovy not finish off his adversary Rotcheff once the latter is wounded? Why does Helena not notify Jean about the fate of her old husband for nearly a year? And why does the villain send his victim to Siberia, thereafter never seeking news of his hoped-for deterioration? L'Amour repeatedly raises reader expectations through primitive foreshadowing, only to avoid following through. For two examples, Jean seeks his father Smoke but never finds him, and a helpful Sitka girl named Dounia kisses Jean energetically but then disappears like smoke. In fact, several of Jean's friends are introduced, sketched with brief strokes, and then dropped like rejected drawings. Perhaps the gravest omission is of that titanic event, the Civil War, which goes virtually unmentioned, as does Abraham Lincoln.

Just Before *The Daybreakers*

L'Amour wrote three more novels before publishing *The Daybreakers* (1960), his first Sackett volume. The three are *Radigan, The First Fast Draw,* and *Taggart*—all published in 1959. None is outstanding.

Tom Radigan, hero of *Radigan*, is yet another honest homesteader trying to improve his life just outside yet another dishonest town. L'Amour tries to ring changes on the formula first by making the opposing would-be land-grabber a corrupt woman backed by both a fraudulent land claim and a crooked crew, and second by offering as love interest young Gretchen, the adopted white daughter of a half-breed Delaware who works for Radigan. Notable in this busy but weak novel are: sweet Gretchen shoving a burning stick into the mouth of an ugly-talking villain, unwittingly luring another bad man to his death when he sniffs too closely after the smell of pie she is baking for her hero, and finally dressing in white as white as flour for that hero's final homecoming.

The First Fast Draw purports to be based on real-life Texas gunman Cullen Montgomery Baker (1835–69). If L'Amour had not pretended that he was writing fictionalized biography, the novel would be just another formulary Western, with minor variations. Thus, the orphaned hero emerges from the Civil War having ridden briefly with William Clarke Quantrill, returns home to northeastern Texas hoping to farm quietly, and falls in love with an attractive young widow named Katy Thorne. Then things go against young Cullen: neighborhood toughs beat him up; Thomas Warren (in real life, Thomas Orr), a weird schoolteacher from New England, woos the widow woman; and Governor Edmund J. Davis's harsh rule turns several anti-Reconstructionists into latter-day guerrillas. These die-hards include Ben Bickerstaff, Matt Kirby, Bob Lee, Bill Longley, and especially their friend Cullen.

So far so good. But L'Amour brings in so many real-life names and adverts to so many real-life post-Civil War activities in Texas that the unwary reader may wrongly conclude that *The First Fast Draw* is an accurate if partly romantic historical reconstruction, which it assuredly is not. L'Amour ignores Baker's first marriage, daughter, wife's death, second marriage, second wife's death, and acts of Quantrill-like violence against freed blacks in Texas and green Union troops there. Instead of having Baker shot to death with Kirby on 6 January 1869, by the schoolteacher and his band, L'Amour has him escape by a clumsy plot strategem, go west with a loyal friend and their lady loves—to marry at last, study law, raise horses, and remember the old days beside the Sulphur River and Lake Caddo. The sunken theme of this novel is thus friendship.

L'Amour does history no service with such a book. His Cullen Baker is about as close to history's gunman as that old Jesse James movie starring Tyrone Power was to history. If L'Amour ever read Eugene Cunningham's 1941 classic *Triggernometry,* he would have noted that Bill Longley was a more feared gunslinger than Baker, and further that it was not Baker but Longley, hanged for murder in 1878, who legend said survived.[13] L'Amour evidently was enamored of Baker, for he mentions him again in *Flint, Mustang Man, The Man from Skibbereen,* and *Bowdrie's Law,* and brings him into the action of *Lando* briefly.

Taggart grew out of L'Amour's clever 1951 short story "Trap of Gold," in which a miner dangerously digs gold out from under a gigantic teetering rock. *Taggart* also features elements from *The Burning Hills* (interracial marriage) and *Last Stand at Papago Wells* (sand storm, confluence of separate groups at a dangerous desert spot in Apacheria). New elements are many. Instead of rivals fighting for lush land, the prize is gold in the harsh desert, long-sought gold about which Spanish legends have long swirled. Bounty hunter pursues justifiably homicidal hero, but soon prefers gold and heroine. Best here is mystical love-atfirst-sound aroused in active hero and patient heroine simultaneously, when the two meet and speak in starlit desert darkness. This represents one of L'Amour's most tender and poetic sequences to date.

After *Taggart* came L'Amour's eighteenth published novel. It is *The Daybreakers* and introduced his ever-widening readership to the famous Sackett dynasty. For variety and also because L'Amour's whole Sackett saga is a great big artistic unit, rather like an enormous hacienda mural, I will treat it, and his Chantry and Talon books as well, in a separate chapter (on family novels) after considering his other novels. Even as L'Amour wrote successive family serials, he was continuing to write separate one-volume formulary and romantic historical reconstructions, as we shall now see.

Chapter Four

L'Amour at High Noon

The Daybreakers (1960), L'Amour's first Sackett novel, concerns brothers Tyrel and Orrin Sackett in 1866–67. It is by no means the earliest Sackett yarn in terms of events. The novel taking up the establishment of the New World Sackett dynasty is *Sackett's Land* (1974), which begins in Elizabethan England in 1599 and features Barnabas Sackett. But these complicated matters, as well as those generated by L'Amour's amorphous Chantry and Talon serials, are best left to a later separate chapter. First, therefore, I want to continue moving through L'Amour's other productions, stressing innovations and downplaying those novels which repeat formulary clichés and previous special effects.

Two Aces

So, next came the superb *Flint* (1960). It was followed by two more Sacketts novels, *Sackett* (1961) and *Lando* (1962).

Flint was voted by the Western Writers of America in a 1977 survey as one of the twenty-five best Westerns of all time (along with *Hondo*).[1] Like *Silver Canyon, Flint* is an anthology of L'Amour's previous plot and character effects, plus a few new tricks. Its plot is unnecessarily complicated. A New Mexican gunman named Flint befriends an orphaned kid named James T. Kettleman, teaches him a lot, finally is shot by a band of men, some of whom the kid kills, while others he only remembers. Years pass, and Jim, now a rich New York businessman, leaves his vicious wife Lottie and returns home by train to die in Flint's malpais hideout of what he thinks is incurable cancer. Hence this novel starts out a trifle like Glendon Swarthout's later novel *The Shootist* (1975). But Kettleman runs smack into a three-sided fight involving: dishonest hand-grabbing railroad magnate (Porter Baldwin), corrupt cattleman (Thomas S. Nugent), and orphaned female rancher (Nancy Kerrigan). Complicating all this are a potent killer (Buckdun) in Baldwin's pay, a man (named Gaddis) who helped shoot Flint and now is a ranchhand under Nancy, the arrival of wife Lottie, and a rediagnosis by a Western doctor of the hero's alleged cancer.

(What do Manhattan medicos know, anyway?) Meanwhile, thugs bad
and reformed wonder if Kettleman, who now calls himself Flint, is the
shot-up gunman miraculously recovered or that fast kid grown up and
bent on revenge.

Flint opens with the hero dropping off a train into the woolly West.
The malpais is marvelously rendered early in the novel, and a villain
falls to his horrible death on its jagged outcroppings late in it. Flint
makes friends with a red stallion. When bad Lottie gloatingly informs
good Nancy that Flint has cancer, the girl's response is unforgettable.
Since the novel has some thirty-five named characters, it is not surprising that L'Amour in his customary compositional haste left some
loose ends: a bodyguard for Nancy simply drops out of sight; a Mexican-American cowboy is billed as a dangerous gun hand but never
proves his prowess; Flint collects his forwarded mail but neglects to
read it; a woman is named and criticized for gossiping, but we never
meet her; and Nancy oddly never learns the truth about Flint's "cancer." It is likely, however, that few readers notice such slips in the
excitement of the many fine touches here: Flint learns to savor life in
the West just when he thinks he is dying; the contrast between Nancy
and Lottie is almost musical; Baldwin's grudging respect for Flint's
boxing ability is a surprise and hence a delight; nature with its beautiful horse, dangerous malpais, and violent rain is wondrously painted;
and L'Amour's whole plot coils like a serpent.

After *Sackett* and *Lando* came *Shalako*, which introduces an intrigu-
ing new element in L'Amour's fictive depiction of the West, that is, a
daintily equipped band of pampered hunters, both European and
American, who have no business in New Mexico with renegade-
Apaches Chato, Machita, and Loco on the prowl in the Sonora Desert
area in April 1882.

The hunting party would be rubbed out fast if it were not for the
hero Shalako Carlin. The party numbers more than twenty people,
including Baron General Frederick Von Hallstatt (veteran of the Franco-Prussian War), Hans Kreuger (Von Hallstatt's underling), Mako
(Von Hallstatt's European chef, brought along because of his fabulous
omelettes), Count Henri (Von Hallstatt's French counterpart, and experienced through having faced African guerrillas), Charles Dagget
(American diplomat), Roy Harding (young Ohio orphan), assorted
Western hunting-party employees displaying loyalty and turpitude,
and four women: Dagget's timorous wife Edna, Laura David (an American senator's daughter), their flirtatious friend Julia Page, and sen-
suous Lady Irina Carnarvon of Wales.[2]

Shalako, Von Hallstatt, and Irina are three of the four most important characters in this crowded novel. The fourth is Tats-ah-das-ay-go,
the Quick Killer, a feared, ghost-silent Apache sneak assassin who kills
to augment his already legendary fame. The army sends separate units
to aid the harrassed whites; but the Quick Killer is superior—as are
the massed Apaches on his side—to all adversaries until. . . . Who
else? Shalako. This man is L'Amour's hero nonpareil. Now aged thirty-
five, he was born in California; grew up on the polyglot Texas frontier
(hence knows French, German, and English); fought in the Civil War
as a Union cavalry officer; went abroad to fight with the Boers in the
Basuto War, then under Shir Ali in Afghanistan, then under Comte
MacMahon from Metz to Bazaine during the Franco-Prussian War.
Next he idled a while in postwar Paris (meeting Edouard Manet, Edgar
Degas, and Emile Zola) and now has been drifting in America's vast
Southwest as free as Zuni winds there. He lectures the camp on a dozen
topics: nature, Indians, horses, women, and even military tactics,
which he learned the hard way but also from such obscure authorities
as Vegetius, Saxe, and Jomini, whom he impresses the European sol-
dier-hunters by naming.[3] Shalako abrasively ridicules Von Hallstatt for
three reasons: he has brought women on a dangerous expedition, is
rank-conscious, and insanely hopes to have "a little brush with" the
Apaches (p. 12).

Among the virtues of *Shalako* are its combat scenes, the character-
defining responses of distinct individuals to danger, and Lady Irina's
growing love for Shalako. The novel is hard to read for two main reasons: each of its four chapters is too long, too dense, and has awkward
shifts in narrative point of view; and there are too many characters for
the plot line to hold. L'Amour seems to want to substitute here, as
elsewhere, complexity and confusion for simpler and therefore more
profound character and action development. What I remember longest
about *Shalako* is Irina's gift to the hero of a noble Arabian steed and
especially the hero's Hemingwayesque respect for his final combat adversary, Tats-ah-das-ay-go, whom he denominates, "almost in anguish,
in admiration: 'Warrior! Brother!'" (p. 167).

A Low Octave

L'Amour's next eight novels show little innovation. With the exception of *How the West Was Won* (1963), each is short, at around 150
pages.

Killoe (1962) is a simple cattle-drive story, with minor switches in routine plotting: the hero has an unstable foster brother who captures the affections of said hero's girlfriend, and the killer is welcome to her; further, the father of the hero turns over leadership of the drive to him. The novel includes effective scenes of violence and dust-eating along the April 1858 trail from Texas to New Mexico, and is punctuated by fine descriptions of desert sounds. But *Killoe* is not recommended for mature audiences.

High Lonesome (1962) does not cut it either. It tries to generate reader sympathy for a prankster-robber who becomes rightly disgusted with himself and seeks to shed the vestigial remains of his past, especially after he meets the lithe heroine and her time-gentled father, a retired wild-bunch member himself. But it is ridiculous for L'Amour to expect us to sympathize with a fellow who plans a bank robbery that his cohorts carry out. We even learn that, long ago, the hero was felonious south of the border; but that was in another country, and besides the Mexican is dead.[4]

I nominate *Fallon* (1963) as L'Amour's poorest novel, perhaps with *The Tall Stranger* and *The Proving Trail* vying for that honor but just losing out. *Fallon* stars a "hero" of the same name who is a card sharp, driven by would-be lynchers from their town and arriving at a deserted town which he tries to lease to profit-inclined merchants subsequently wagoning in with goods for sale to still later arrivals. Events taxing on reader patience pile one on another to such an extent that I would argue that L'Amour is here striving for satire of the Western novel except that satire is of absolutely no moment to him.

Next came *How the West Was Won* (1963), which, as adapted from the film script of James R. Webb, becomes a five-act dramatic epic. The labeled parts are "The Rivers," "The Plains," "The [Civil] War," "The Iron Horse," and "The Outlaws." Most Western buffs should remember the movie, with its tremendous cast—at least eighteen first-rate actors and actresses. But some movie buffs—and critics—wrongly think to this day that the cinerama extravaganza followed L'Amour's book.

All the same, L'Amour ably narrates the aid which fur-trapper Linus Rawlings (James Stewart in the movie) gives the Prescott and Harvey families, who are in danger on the turbulent Ohio River around 1840. Lilith Prescott (Debbie Reynolds) accepts some money from Rawlings and heads west, to a career as actress, wife, then peppy surrogate matriarch. Her older sister Eve (Carol Baker) marries Rawlings, who does not survive Shiloh (1862), although their son Zebulon (George Peppard) does, after which he too goes west, staying in the army and meeting a mountain man and his family. The last part carries us forward to 1883.

This is the barest skeleton of the plot, which stretches across a continent and includes activities of four generations of pioneering stock. Eve, the daughter of Zebulon Prescott (Karl Malden) and his wife (Agnes Moorhead), marries Rawlings; Zebulon, one of their four offspring, is the father of Prescott, Linus, and Eve. For all the world, we have here a TV mini-series before its time. It is possible that the *Roots*-like nature of its multigenerational story lines encouraged L'Amour to continue his Sackett series, which by 1963 numbered only three volumes.[5]

Abijah "Bijah" Catlow is the hero of *Catlow* (1963) and, like many other Western outlaws in reality and in fiction, was legally innocent of any wrongdoing. But an ungrateful former boss and a dishonest lawman tried without success to frame and hang him for rustling. Bijah escapes and aids his boyhood friend Ben Cowan, now a deputy marshal. So we have an "outlaw" who in reality is good, and a lawman who seems "bad" through association. They are "never quite friends, never quite enemies; always a respect, each for the other" (p. 88).

The improbable plot—a chase for $2,000,000 in lost Benito Juarez gold—carries Bijah and Ben south of the border deep into Mexico, and makes them acquainted with matching heroines, for romantic balance. (Each man will name his first son for the other.) The faithful white heroine is named Cordelia, while the resourceful Hispanic woman, Rosita, mentions gratuitously that her cousin is lawman Tyrel Sackett's wife up in Mora, New Mexico.[6]

In *Dark Canyon* (1963), as in many earlier novels, L'Amour substitutes plot complications for narrow profundity. At one point there are eight distinct lines of action aimed at the young hero's ranch. That hero, Gaylord Riley, is hardly out of his teens and wants to quit a life of crime. So his older partners provide funds for him to start a ranch with a white-face herd near Dark Canyon, by Fable Canyon, near the Sweet Alice Hills beside the Painted Desert. But, as is often the case in L'Amour, the newcomer is opposed by villains in themselves rivals for land and the girl. In return for use of the tainted money from his former cronies, Riley has promised to offer them sanctuary if needed. Need naturally comes, and so does Tell Sackett—for no reason whatsoever save that L'Amour then wished to keep the name Sackett before his readers' eyes pending release of *Mojave Crossing, The Sackett Brand, Mustang Man,* etc.

I wish that L'Amour had chosen to make something of the symbolism latent in the name Dark Canyon. Also, he might have philosophized to more effect on the relativity of evil here. After all, Riley's solid fortune is built over the dark canyons of stolen funds.

Hanging Woman Creek (1964) includes a train ride west (as in *Flint*), the challenge of life in brutally cold 1885 Montana (see *Heller with a Gun*), naive Europeans entering the harsh West (*Shalako*), and an improbably fast land-bequeathing (*Utah Blaine, Silver Canyon*). New in *Hanging Woman Creek,* however, are two fine elements: the hero, Barney "Pronto" Pike, though honest, is a feisty, drifting loser reluctant to reform, while the catalyst speeding his self-improvement is a well-delineated black man named Eddie Holt, who becomes Pronto's partner, boxing instructor, and mentor. Old by now also is Pronto's being caught between evil rivals: cattle barons with vigilante-style hired killers vs. harmless nesters. Montana heroes Granville Stuart and X. Beidler are mentioned but never touched into reality. Nice and new here is a unique kind of villainess—a wandering, demented woman whose motivation is hopelessly askew yet fascinating. Again, something should have been made of the title's latent symbolism. As it is, the title is totally useless.

Conn Dury is overqualified to be the hero of the mistitled *Kiowa Trail* (1964). L'Amour must have realized that the main action of this short novel was perilously thin. It concerns the strangling blockade of a Kansas town by cattle-driving Texas cowboys, because one of their number has been murdered there. So L'Amour includes a sequence of six flashbacks out of chronological order but in a dramatic crescendo. The present situation is this: Kate Lundy is a rich widow, owns the Texas herd in question, and is driving it north with her nineteen-year-old brother Tom as a member of her crew. Her trail boss is Dury. Young Tom violates the curfew of the sanctimonious town by visiting a depraved young manteaser who wants to have him killed so as to enhance her reputation. And it happens.

For revenge Kate leases adjacent railroad land, fences the town in, and prepares to destroy it by blocking all commercial lines in and out. Meanwhile, we read in the flashbacks that Dury is a trifle like Tarzan: orphaned by an Indian massacre, he lived among Apaches, was saved by a traveling British officer named James Sotherton, whose friendship and then murder led Dury (after incomplete revenge) to England to meet Sotherton's father Sir Richard—to attend school there and travel on the Continent. Home again in America, he wandered Western gold fields, became a Texas Ranger, got into trouble in Mexico, rode north and happened by to save Kate and Tom from an Apache attack that killed her husband, then after service in the Union army during the Civil War returned to Kate as an employee.

The only significant connection between Dury's zestful past and Kate's present determination to choke the Kansas town is the fact that the one surviving killer of Sotherton is now there.

This summary only begins to trace the outlines of a plot too heavy for a 148-page story. The flashbacks are more exciting than its present action, although L'Amour complicates the present quite well. If the strands of the two plots were pulled out and rewoven in chronological order, we would have action covering decades in the life of its thirty-five-year-old hero; but L'Amour, for his own unknown reasons, chose otherwise, avoided following that hero through the Civil War, and gives us instead one of his most unusual structures.

Seven More

Of the next seven books, two more concern Sacketts. Both are narrated by and star redoubtable Tell Sackett. They are *Mojave Crossing* (1964) and *The Sackett Brand* (1965).

The following five other novels are *The High Graders* (1965), *The Key-Lock Man* (1965), *The Broken Gun* (1966), *Kid Rodelo* (1966), and *Kilrone* (1966). The middle one is clearly the best.

The High Graders stars yet another lark-loving criminal (as did *High Lonesome*), here a reformed rustler who returns home and becomes so honest even when associating with former dishonest friends that he kills a few. Killing? Yes, eleven in the course of the action, enacted in and near a mining town run, as is often the case in L'Amour's fiction, by crooked leaders—especially, here, by high-graders. They are mine-owners and merchants who assay gold ore at low rates and ship it out for higher resale. New here is the shooting to death of a crooked woman by irate miners. A charming symbolic touch is provided when filthy water from the gold mines pollutes the source of drinking water for cattle: modern technology ruins an age-old natural process. L'Amour will use again this story's scariest situation: being trapped in a deep, dark mine shaft.

The hero of *The Key-Lock Man* is Matt Keylock, who though innocent of crime is pursued by six possemen of various degrees of toughness and misgivings. The opening comic tone (reminiscent of *Fallon*)
gives way to a somber tone once the heroine is introduced: European
born and a veritable Viking, Kristina killed her lover for the best of
reasons but then had to flee to America. She did so by answering an
ad for a mail-order bride, then objected to the villain she reported to
in the so-called virgin land of the West. Enter Mr. Keelock, already
Kristina's Western husband. Further to tighten already knotted plot
lines is the introduction of a train of wagons laden with California gold
lost somewhere in the Painted Desert region of Arizona or Utah.

Then came the best of this group of books, and one of L'Amour's
most unusual novels to date—*The Broken Gun,* so far his only full-
length fictional effort cast in the twentieth century. Yet it too is a
Western—with rugged Western hero, Hispanic helper figure, cooperative lawman, squad of land-greedy villains, comely heroine in distress, vixeny villainess, messages by telephone rather than by smoke
signal, quick transportation by jeep as well as by horse—all in remote
stretches of southeastern Arizona. Everything starts when L'Amour's
most autobiographical hero, combat veteran and Western-writer Dan
Sheridan, finds a Toomey family journal dating back to the 1870s
stuffed into the barrel of a broken Bisley Colt he bought in New Orleans about 1962. Its message leads Sheridan to investigate land fraud-
ulently held by descendants of killers of said Toomeys.

Nothing is very new about the main elements of the action: villain
invites hero to his ranch and hence into his clutches, upfront hero arms
enemy by boasting of his evidence and intentions, hero escapes murderous trap in mountains, hero takes evasive action and joins heroine.
She is temporarily captured while hero is on the loose, being helped
by canny native. Stock properties include fire, pusillanimous neighbors, assorted fights (including obligatory fistfight[7]), arrival of law,
location of long-lost needful documents. The charm of *The Broken Gun*
lies not in any story line with time-honored Gothic ingredients, but
in L'Amour's delightful translation of them into twentieth-century
terms. The memorable result reminds me of an earlier novel by Ernest
Haycox entitled *The Silver Desert* (1935), and Henry W. Allen's later
Tayopa! (1970).

For a change, *Kid Rodelo* is a novel with a simple plot. Released from
Yuma Prison for a gold robbery that he did not commit, Rodelo joins
a team of thugs (led by the friend who sent him to prison as a jest) on
a sandy mission south of the border to pick up said gold. After all, the

Kid did time for it. We soon have a situation not too remote from that of B. Traven's classic *The Treasure of the Sierra Madre*. Partial regeneration through suffering is the main theme.

Kilrone is L'Amour's earliest thoroughgoing treatment of military life in the West. Much in it is standard: glory-seeking commanding officer; Indians of various degrees of sneakiness and ineptitude; dissolute but very tough white villain, from the East and out in the West to make money—by providing the post with cards, whiskey, and women, and the Indians with whiskey and guns; long-suffering wives on the post; army payroll being dangerously wagoned in to the already under-manned post; and remarkable hero with a past so varied that he is now equal to any situation.

But much in *Kilrone* is also fresh and different. The hero is Barnes Kilrone, West Pointer and former official American military observer abroad during the Franco-Prussian War. The time is now vaguely after the Battle of the Rosebud (1876) and Chief Joseph's brave but tragic retreat (1877). Kilrone, now a civilian, reports to the post in northern Nevada that Bannock Indians in the rugged region have wiped out a patrol under the colonel. But the acting commander, Major Frank Paddock, disbelieves Kilrone because when the two men were in Paris as war observers together they disputed over the affections of one Denise de Caslou. Although Paddock won her hand in marriage (hence the hero though thirty-two years of age is still single), he feels that Denise lingeringly pines for Kilrone. This is untrue, since the woman is happy and loves the American West. Not surprisingly, Denise has a gorgeous female friend on the post; she is Betty Considine, niece of the post surgeon, who falls in love with Kilrone faster than in a Hollywood love story. Before he can propose to her in a way typical of L'Amour—"Ever been to California? . . . It's a nice place for a honeymoon" (p. 152)—trouble must be wheeled out and driven at the reader. The novel is nicely balanced in a way traditional critics of the formulary Western would approve: scenes within the post give way to scenes of pursuit outside, pursuit complicated in the old-fashioned way whereby aggressive white soldiers often become redskins' quarry.[8] The topography in which such maneuvers take place is especially well described.

Two More Sacketts in a Sack of Seven

By this time, L'Amour had become skillful in platooning Sacketts and non-Sacketts in commercially winning formations. Thus, among the next seven books come two new Sackett segments. They are *Mus-*

tang Man (1966) and *The Sky-Liners* (1967), each introducing a new
Sackett cousin for Tell and his brothers, and both featuring lost gold.
Fresher in plotting are some of the other five, which are *Matagorda*
(1967), *Down the Long Hills* (1968), *Chancy* (1968), *Brionne* (1968),
and *The Empty Land* (1969).

Matagorda contains L'Amour's best evocation of place, and it is
therefore well titled.[9] The hero Tappan "Tap" Duvarney, veteran on the
Union side of the Civil War and then an Indian fighter, now wants to
join forces with his partner Tom Kittery from anti-Yankee Texas in a
cattle venture. But touchy Tom, whom Tap captured during the war
and then befriended, prefers feuding against the rival Munson family
instead of cowboying with Tap from Matagorda up to Dodge City. So
do several of Tom's hotblooded hands. Thus L'Amour's hero here steps
not into a range war, as earlier heroes have done, but into a bloody
Southern feud. Fine innovation, so far. And the author commendably
complicates things by introducing a contrasting pair of women. One
is Jessica, Tap's loyal Virginia fiancée; the other is Mady, Tom's fiancée,
who is as modern in her addiction to city lights as Jessica is traditional
in deferring to male authority. The novel also includes as cold and
curious a villain as L'Amour ever invented. He is pro-Munson Jackson
Huddy, a cowardly backshooter, but also a churchgoer and a great re-
specter of womenfolk.

Matagorda has half a dozen defects. We have a weird pair of brothers
named Lightly and Darkly Foster who are in the story mainly for the
humor of those names. Eight hundred cows and three cowboys get up,
break camp, and depart, while the hero peacefully sleeps through all
the noise. Tom is described as heroic in the feud, but during the action
catching Tap in its toils is mostly either inept or absent. The solid
courthouse is too tardily thought of as a refuge against graphically
described flood waters. The Munson faction sits to one side and lets
the good guys rescue flood victims, then resumes lethal warfare against
them. And L'Amour seems too ready—as are many other conservative
Western writers—to consider murder properly forgotten once it is
nominally avenged, and also to let female wrongdoers off with a mere
wrist slap. But one symbolic action makes up for all weaknesses here.
Lovely Jessica, whose appearance at exactly the half-way point of the
novel shifts the action into a new key, loses to the flood every tangible
shred of her aristocratic past—family pictures, books, clothes, and the
like. She is thus dramatically imaged as giving her all to follow her
man into the rugged West and a new life.

Down the Long Hills is unlike anything else L'Amour ever wrote. It is remarkably unified in time, place, and action. In September 1848 seven-year-old Hardy Collins must walk west through cold Wyoming hills toward Fort Bridger and in the process save his little companion, three-year-old Betty Sue Powell. (Each is a little too young for what follows.) All the adults of the wagon train carrying them west have been massacred by Comanches. Young Hardy, well schooled in wood-craft and hunting by his widowered father Scott,[10] is equal to the task, but only barely—because opposing him are three enemy forces: an Indian who covets the boy's stallion, a mutilated bear named Old Three Paws, and a pair of white thugs fresh from an early tour of robbery in the California gold fields. But also closing in, to bring aid, are Hardy's father and two friendly mountain men, who return from the fort area, having gone on ahead of the wagon train earlier. So, in this pursuit, evasion, and rescue narrative we have five diagrammable lines of action. Narrative unity is intensified by the unusually small number of characters—only eight—in the story.

The short novel is a handbook on wilderness survival. The best features are Hardy's resourcefulness, the depiction of a superstitious Indian, the thugs' shades of villainy, the two fine animals, and the father's confident love for his child. The novel could have used some polyphonic variety: L'Amour's concentration on cold, hunger, fatigue, and fear is unrelieved. Further, I wish that L'Amour might somehow have violated the compelling use of the child's point of view far fewer times. Often he shifts to the point of view of one or another adult, necessarily, I suppose, given his plot lines. But at one point he awkwardly tells us that "The Indian did not, as yet, realize that he, too, was followed" (p. 44).

Chancy is mostly an unpleasant combination of old plot ingredients making up yet another formulary Western. In it a fatherless young drifter (as in *To Tame a Land*), who is hated by his neighbors (see *The First Fast Draw, Lando*) and who has been to sea (*Crossfire Trail, Sitka*), gains rights to a cattle herd very fast (*Killoe*) and is too happy-go-lucky for his own good (*Fallon, The Key-Lock Man*). A gun provides evidence (*The Broken Gun*), and the evil force is feminine (*Radigan*). A good young woman travels far to meet the hero (*Matagorda*). *Chancy* starts off well but is marred not only by familiar plot elements, as noted, but also by improbable climaxing.

Brionne begins with a fresh situation but is ruinously hasty in execution. The hero is James Brionne, who like Shalako and Kilrone is a former military man of Western and European experience, and who is now a reluctant statesman in Washington, D.C., and is also a husband and the father of a son (Mat) not quite seven years old. How to get the two males west? Have the lovely wife and mother assaulted at home before her boy's very eyes and while her husband is away. She resists the villains, kills one, and commits suicide to avoid a fate worse than death; and the other thugs flee. Brionne seeks revenge without success, must get away for a second chance, and hopes to give his now chronically shocked little son a new beginning in that best of environments, the Far West. Would you guess that Brionne and Mat, once they get to Cheyenne and Promontory and into the rugged regions beyond, might find not only that second chance but also a second wife, a second mother, maybe even silver in the mountains, and perhaps the ragged remnants of the gang of would-be rapists from back home? A clever historical touch is Brionne's conferring briefly in St. Louis with U. S. Grant.

In *The Empty Land* L'Amour presents the early days of a tough town, somewhat of the sort presented in *Fallon* and *The High Graders.* The town—aptly christened Confusion—grows too fast once gold is discovered in what become its outskirts. A miner who has discovered the gold thinks naively that reason and not guns can talk to and govern the lawless thugs who descend on the region for loot. Not likely. So the decent element must appeal to wearily experienced Matt Coburn, who happens by but is reluctant to become Confusion's lawman. L'Amour adopts a fatalistic tone here: obliged to rescue and then have dinner with a beautiful woman who is riskily ranching hereabouts, then hear how thugs murdered an early town marshal, and finally help a rich traveling actress who stagecoaches in, Matt is inevitably caged both by circumstances and also by his own temperament. As in an old Errol Flynn movie, behold hero Matt Coburn resolutely strapping on his guns, which he is all too adept at wielding. Adept? Well, he posts a list of the seventy most unwanted men in Confusion, and by jerky stages expels all but the die-hard ten percent or so he naturalistically kills. The novel has plot complexities unhinted at here, and moreover all in quick time with the lightning impressionism of a Shakespearean history play. *The Empty Land* is memorable for the reluctance of its hero, his willingness to nurture the psychological development of a few wavering young persons, and also the differing responses to needful heroic violence registered by the two distinct heroines.

Sextet with Three Themes

Of the next six novels, two—*The Lonely Men* (1969) and *Galloway* (1970)—are Sacketts, three play variations on old motifs, and the last introduces the name Chantry to L'Amourdom. *The Lonely Men* takes Tell Sackett and a crew deep into Apacheria, while *Galloway* continues adventures of two of Tell's cousins introduced in *The Sky-Liners*. The four non-Sackett novels here are *Conagher* (1969), *The Man Called Noon* (1970), *Reilly's Luck* (1970), and *North to the Rails* (1971).

Conagher is named after its hero, a middle-aged Civil War veteran who is tired of fighting and drifting, and is eager for a home. But the uniquely memorable character in the novel is the touching heroine, young Evie Teale, widowed when her nice old juiceless husband dies in the desert and leaves her with his two kids (from a former marriage) to support by trying to manage a New Mexico stagecoach station.

L'Amour brilliantly characterizes this young woman, as well as some other females in what becomes a charmingly relevant depiction of life from their point of view in the harsh West of yesteryear. Evie's two stepchildren are sturdy Laban (an eleven-year-old boy) and Ruthie (younger but with age unspecified, snippy at first but a girl whom the West improves fast). Into the scene come two adult females: one is Lucy, who seeks her outlaw brother, on the run from Philadelphia; the other is their Aunt Celestine, who merely accompanies Lucy. L'Amour poignantly dramatizes the failure of Lucy and Celestine ever to find the lost brother and nephew. We have a mere glimpse of another type of woman, too. She is a tough young one, aboard a coach stopping only a moment, with some wounded men whom she tends carefully. Then away again, as in life all too often. But most touching is Evie, who like Herman Melville's Hunilla (in *The Encantadas*) is protected by an armor of toughness that shields undying gentleness within. She traces a floral pattern on her dirt floor, to make it appear carpeted. And she writes out sentimental little messages and mails them on drifting tumbleweeds, hoping that her knight in shining chaps will come for her.

As in earlier fiction, the hero here tries to help two young men. He saves one, but the other chooses the darker trail. And again as in earlier stories, Indians nearby could make awful trouble for the heroine, but they admire her spunk too much for that. And as before, we have a nearby rancher, itinerant rustlers, an unimportant town with saloon and law in the distance. In short, *Conagher* is a formulary Western with some commendable women's-liberation twists.

Late in the novel called *The Man Called Noon* we learn that Eastern Jonas Mandrin, former correspondent, author, arms expert, arms-company founder and owner, hunter, and world traveler, lost his wife and child, changed his name to Ruble Noon, hired out to Tom Davidge to come west and rid him of some evil people squeezing his ranch. We read early in the novel, however, that one of those villains shoots Noon in the head, causing amnesia. Yes, just as in Clay Fisher's earlier *Return of the Tall Man* (1961) and Luke Short's later *The Stalkers* (1973), *The Man Called Noon* employs amnesia, one of the most upsetting of plot nutrients. And yet with great subtlety L'Amour has the past gradually emerge from the hero's clouded inner vision as events rush his endangered new identity through horrible crises toward a future improved not only by returning memory but also by dead Tom's gorgeous daughter Fan Davidge.

The Man Called Noon has L'Amour's most complicated plot. It is a tangle of narrative difficulties, the threads of which are impossible to summarize, let alone sort out in one's mind. We have railroad car and cave, gangs of rival crooks, enigmatic letters, mountain cabin, escape route by shaft in mountain rocks, ambushes by ranch and saloon, midnight rendezvous in absent lawyer's office, evil female and greedy judge, loyal Mexican stableman, research into newspaper files, rescue of condemned Mexican husband of fine woman, mini-avalanche, phenomenal marksmanship, escape through underground passage, treasure map, tree house, strongbox with deeds and currency, train ride and shootout. For all the world, this novel reads like L'Amour's parody of L'Amour. Although in retrospect its excesses are ludicrous, it is captivating on first reading.

By the time of *Reilly's Luck,* L'Amour was thoroughly in possession of his narrative talents and sometimes shopworn subject matter. This novel is accordingly a vivid combination of previous themes plus some variations. *Reilly's Luck* is big, like *Sitka,* with temporal and geographical spread. Will Reilly's "luck" is his adopted boy Valentine "Val" Darrant, who as an unwanted child is marked by his unprincipled mother Myra Cord for murder but who is saved, nurtured, and grows up to become the story's hero. This concentration on training a youngster is reminiscent of *Hondo, To Tame a Land, Flint, Kiowa Trail, Down the Long Hills,* and *Brionne.* But the training is different here! Reilly is a sharp card player, an expert marksman, an associate of shady Westerners of sundry types, a reader, and a foreign traveler. So Val soon becomes knowledgeable concerning poker, books, fists, guns, criminals, and Europe—especially Austria, but also the Alps, Zurich, Paris, London, Philadelphia, and New York. After a teen-aged tour of duty as a Texas cowboy, he rejoins Reilly briefly, until the latter is murdered—by a trio paid by Prince Pavel, a Russian gambler who would have profitably married off his beautiful cousin Princess Louise but for handsome Reilly's intervention back there in Innsbruck. Val's juvenile travels permit us to compare the young man to several previous L'Amour heroes, while the Russian villain smacks specifically of *Sitka*.

L'Amour bends probability, once Val completes some of his wander-years (undertaking partial revenge, salvage work in the Mississippi River, law study in New York, and love in the West again). Prince Pavel (with sweet loser Louise along) meets in New York Val's evil mother Myra, now rich, widowed, and doubly venomous through both commercial ambition and fear because she now knows that her son is alive and sturdy. They then come to the West to consummate dastardly machinations. Chapter 23 is a masterpiece of plot-line vectoring, as nine main characters prepare for battle, all meeting at the new Windsor Hotel in Denver in the early 1880s.

The novel has enough action for nine hours of TV prime time. There are more than 120 characters in it, counting deceased persons whose actions are significant to the plot and counting historical persons as well (for example, financier James Hill, Billy the Kid, and French painter Robert Fleury). I wish that its twenty-seven chapters could be seen as falling into symmetrical fractions—say, thirds—but they simply sprawl instead. At about the one-quarter mark, Reilly is killed. At the halfway point, Val's mother hires real-life Allen Pinkerton, and the plot pivots ponderously. At about the three-quarter spot the Prince and his party head west for his shocking comeuppance. Plot lines sadly trail off in midchapter, and on a couple of occasions Val's point of view is awkwardly eclipsed. In fact, *Reilly's Luck* has at least a dozen authorial slips. For example, the heroine, whose first name is Boston, says that she is spoken for but is not. A man named Dube becomes Duke, while a villain named Pike become Peck (not to be confused with another man in the story also named Peck). A letter is delivered to the wrong post office, so that Val can pick it up there. Myra fancies that she can inherit her abandoned son's property. (Surely lawyer Val could make a will cutting her out.) Val rushes to marry Boston to make her his heiress, but neglects to write his will and even postpones their wedding to make it a family affair. A renowned pugilist tells Val that they should do some sparring, but we never see them doing so. We read that Val never saw Wild Bill Hickok again; then he sees him again.[11] Joe Slade becomes Jack Slade.

North to the Rails is an undistinguished Western and would not be worth much extended discussion here except for the fact that it is the first to be published of what promises to be an extensive series of novels devoted to L'Amour's Chantry family. Oddly, in *North to the Rails* we meet Tom Chantry, the son of Borden Chantry, hero of *Borden Chantry*, which was published half a dozen years later. I can see no useful purpose in L'Amour's thus timing the release of these Chantry volumes.

North to the Rails is a cattle-drive story, rendered different through the hero's initial belief (like the pacifist thinking in *The Empty Land*) that he need not use guns in the reasonable West. We also have another unprincipled villainess. The plot features a tepid nonlove story, the heroine of which contributes zero to the action and only poignancy to the tone. Silliest is Tom's making a substantial bet with a canny thug on the trail north that he can last the duration. Is that not like a thirsty man betting a prostitute that she cannot get him drunk and then kill him? The novel is rousing but wobbly.

Chapter Five
L'Amour at Sunset

L'Amour faced the 1970s in full possession of his storytelling powers. *North to the Rails* was his fiftieth novel. By this time he had well introduced his reading public to his Sackett clan and his Chantrys. The Talon family must also have been firmly in his mind. In addition, he was planning many more formulary novels and romantic historical reconstructions.

Six More, Including Sacketts and a Chantry

L'Amour's next six novels were *Under the Sweetwater Rim* (1971), *Tucker* (1971), *Callaghen* (1972), two more Sackett sagas—*Ride the Dark Trail* (1972) and *Treasure Mountain* (1972)—plus *The Ferguson Rifle* (1973), which deals with a very early nineteenth-century Chantry. The narrator of *Ride the Dark Trail* is Logan Sackett, another cousin of Tell and his brothers. *Treasure Mountain* details Tell's and Orrin's efforts to trace their lost father's final days. *The Ferguson Rifle* is narrated by a new Chantry, named Ronan Chantry, who like several earlier L'Amour heroes is saddened by events in the East (including his wife's death) and who, heading west for regeneration, finds with it male companionship, adventure, danger, gold, and romance.

Under the Sweetwater Rim combines much that is familiar with a few new elements. As in *Shalako* and *Kilrone,* its hero is a military man with American and European army experience, while, as in *Catlow,* two central male figures, once friends, are now on opposite sides of the law. Further, the present hero, like a dozen from L'Amour's past fiction, is shot in the skull and thus unhorsed, then falls to miraculous safety in concealing vegetation. As usual, the plot is complex, too much so even when one considers that the novel is longer than L'Amour's average up to this point. An army hero, on leave, is disliked by his commanding officer, whose reputation he saves and whose daughter he loves. *Under the Sweetwater Rim* has twenty-one jumpy chapters, with narrative points of view unbelievably inchoate. The title seems poor, since the action moves west of Fort Laramie toward Fort

Bridger and South Pass City. The time is specified as April 1864; yet hints are also given that the Civil War is over.

Tucker is a simple story about a hero in his teens, seeking to avenge the death of his father on the cattle trail and to recover funds advanced by Texas neighbors to finance the herd. Desire for revenge takes young Shell Tucker, who is like the heroes of *To Tame a Land* and *Chancy,* across dangerous terrain, again as in *To Tame a Land,* and on to California (see *Mojave Crossing* and *The Sackett Brand*), but more importantly to an awareness that violence begets violence and that revenge can ruin its seeker. The finest feature of this picaresque ramble is L'Amour's skill in manipulating events so that his hero is willing to back off and commits himself to violence only in justifiable reaction.

Callaghen, like *Kilrone* and *Under the Sweetwater Rim,* is an army novel but with a brilliant plot twist and other neat features that make it a first-rate action story. It seems that an impostor, posing as an army lieutenant ordered to a Southwestern post, enters the region with a concealed map to a river of gold. He rashly takes a command into the Mojave Desert but is killed there by hostile Indians. Now enter the hero. He is versatile, Irish-born Mort Callaghen, with a soldier-of-fortune past that includes duty in the Middle East, Afghanistan, and China. He must find that map, and discomfit the new, anti-Irish commanding officer (Major Ephraim Sykes) who comes in to replace the decent former one. Callaghen must also save various patrols foolishly ordered into the merciless desert, and also merit the love of a heroine who fortuitously happens by from Los Angeles.

Callaghen is exciting, with a big cast of characters, and with the now expected tangle of plot lines and point-of-view shifts. One comic note: Sykes gained his Civil War fame because he charged the enemy but only when his horse ran wild. (Shades of Mark Twain's hilarious 1891 story entitled "Luck.") A finer touch comes when hero and heroine decide that a single-minded search for gold can be injurious to your spiritual health.

Next? *The Ferguson Rifle.* It is yet another narrative about seeking lost gold, Mexican this time, as in *Lando*—to name one L'Amour precedent. But this novel, featuring a bookish hero, Ronan "Scholar" Chantry,[1] and cast immediately after the Louisiana Purchase, takes on new coloration and points toward *Over on the Dry Side* and *Rivers West.* Ronan is the earliest Chantry thus far in respect to time of action. And in *The Ferguson Rifle* are hints as to his Irish family connections that tease the reader into hoping for Chantry follow-ups. Further, the oddly named villain, Rafen Falvey, takes on mythic dimensions that help prepare the reader for such later melodramatic types as Barnabas Sackett and his doughty cohorts, and also Tatton Chantry. The heroine of *The Ferguson Rifle* is a damsel-in-distress teenager, most attractive, for sure; but would an eight-man party, bent on securing a fortune through furs, give up their direct route to it so as to escort her from the Dakotas to Canada, on her way back to Ireland and home again? Oddly, the titular rifle does less for the hero than a millenium-old knife from India—another touch from *Lando*.

Three Strange Rescuers

The Man from Skibbereen (1973), *The Quick and the Dead* (1973), and *The Californios* (1974) feature three different men, each on a rescue mission. Crispin "Cris" Mayo from Skibbereen, Ireland, gets jilted at home and migrates to America, to work on the railroad. But he is abandoned by mistake out west and becomes an innocent witness to a conspiracy to kill some post-Civil War generals, including William Tecumseh Sherman and Philip Sheridan, hunting in Wyoming Territory in 1868. *The Quick and the Dead* features a splendid wagons-west hero who comes to the aid of a good man and his fine wife. This action is unusual here, since our hero could easily fall in love with that other man's wife. And in *The Californios* a Mexican-Irish sailor returns from the sea to aid his mother, in danger of losing her California home. The son can rescue her only with the miraculous intervention of an immemorially old Hispanic friend and his ghostly Indian confreres. In these three novels, L'Amour is clearly combining old ingredients with startlingly new ones.

Cris Mayo, who is *The Man from Skibbereen*, is an engaging lad. Being from Ireland in the nineteenth century, he knows horses[2] and fisticuffs. But he becomes adept too fast in the use of Western firearms. In spite of having a fingertip recently shot off, Cris enters a boxing contest that provides him a stake to venture on to California, to raise horses there, and surely to start a home and a family with the willing heroine. The hero is caught up in well-paced action first, however, with credibly timed incidents. (Perhaps a bit too much occurs in one long October week.) Cris becomes Americanized in a rush, forgetting his female Irish flame, ignoring his ambition to return rich to the Old World to gloat, and coming under the spell of the enchanting Far West. Cris soon aches for a home of his own there, and, sensing that it is within reach, offers this soliloquy, which is the finest passage in *The Man from Skibbereen:* "Let us not lose this, . . . let us not lose this, God, for there is no greater beauty . . ." (p. 159). Cris is an unusual L'Amour hero for taking the offensive without pause, for boasting of his prowess, and for an outlook too sunny and optimistic for the circumstances. The novel is oddly marred by a duet and trio of names confusingly close: thus we have Parry and Parley, and Barda, Barnes, and Barney.

In *The Quick and the Dead,* once Duncan McKaskel and his wife Susanna, both Easterners wagoning west about 1858 with their twelve-year-old son Tom, pass a loyalty test before the glinting gaze of hero Con Vallian, he backs them all—but in ways that strengthen their independence. Like the hero of *Hondo,* Con trains his sexual rival's little boy. And as in other earlier works, we have here an Indian whose animosity vacillates, then is nullified when he sees the heroine's courage in action. L'Amour evidently flirted at this point in his career with the possibility of off-color incidents. The second villain, a sensualist, announces his desire to kill both Con and Duncan, then torture Susanna, then rape her. Perhaps L'Amour also succumbed here to the temptation to use too much violence: in the last chapter of *The Quick and the Dead* Con shoots a third villain just above his belt buckle and then just under his right eye. Next comes the main violence: to rid the happy homesteading McKaskel of the brawny sensualist, Con must shoot him—count 'em—in chest, arm, leg, then somewhere else three more times. L'Amour exaggerates the Western code of fair play by the hero when he has Duncan, armed with a rifle at the window of his threatened home, simply watch the one-on-one gunplay.

The Quick and the Dead is marred by some of L'Amour's most atrocious grammar. We are treated to the following: "The Huron had shot at what he believed was him . . ."; "no one [was] sure of he who rode beside him"; and "Searching for Vallian, whom he knew was somewhere near. . ." (pp. 71, 145, 164).

The Californios is one of L'Amour's most unusual works, until, at least, *The Lonesome Gods,* which through its pervasive mysticism it partly resembles. Its hero is Sean Mulkerin, swashbuckling, twenty-two-year-old son of red-haired Eileen of Ireland and deceased Irish-Mexican Jaime Mulkerin, once of the Mexican army. Their other son is a monk named Michael, who can use a rifle all right but prefers to pray. Sean needs more than prayers to help their mother keep her Malibu ranch from greedy Yankee landgrabbers in 1844. To add to his gallery of enemies, L'Amour encourages Sean to rescue Mariana de la Cruz from the clutches of greasy-evil Andres Machado, her fiery fiancé, whom she never wanted—this down in Acapulco harbor as Sean sets sail for California with too little cargo in furs to bail out his mother.

What Sean needs is the aid not only of centegenarian Juan, his mystic surrogate father, but also of Juan's nonmaterial Indian helpers whose sandals whisper tracklessly in the sand, and back and forth across time itself. A high point is L'Amour's making a symbol for the time barrier out of shimmering heat waves rising from the desert. What happens in one week to the healthy if cruel face of one villain who tampers with old Juan might inspire some of Hollywood's best horror-makeup artists. *The Californios* has more than its quota of familiar ingredients—women in distress, Yankees threatening Hispanics, resourceful sailor now on horseback, honorable natives, danger in the hot desert and cold mountains, elusive gold, hard fists, Los Angeles in its early days, remote caves, skull-shot hero, and much historical background. What is new and highly memorable is old Juan, with the bag of tricks he plays—in warped time.

Six, Mostly in Extenuation

Of the next six novels, three add details to the ongoing Sackett series, one is the first Talon novel, one is another Chantry installment, and one—as noted much earlier—tells us more about legend-maker Kilkenny.

The next Sacketts are *Sackett's Land* (1974), which introduces us to dynasty-founder Barnabas Sackett; *The Man from the Broken Hills* (1975), nominally a Sackett novel but starring Milo Talon, hence really a Talon book; and *To the Far Blue Mountains* (1976), a continuation of Barnabas's New World adventures. *Rivers West* (1975) tells us how Jean Daniel Talon departs the gorgeous Gaspé Peninsula in northeast Canada in 1821 to trek southwest and west, building and exploring as he proceeds to Maine, Albany, Pittsburgh, St. Louis, and beyond. *Over on the Dry Side* (1975) grafts yet another account of a widower and his educable son, as they homestead in Colorado, onto the touching story of Owen Chantry's arrival at that homestead site—really his house and land—for the purpose of finding a family treasure hidden thereabouts. And *The Rider of Lost Creek* (1976) continues the derring-do story of Kilkenny, here summoned to Texas to break up a ranch war between Lords and Steeles, whose squabble is caused by neither faction but rather by an Eastern villain eager to pick up the pieces, which just might include Nita Riordan, Kilkenny's undying, unsatisfied love.

Rivers West is a supermelodramatic period piece. It turns on the scheme of master-villain Colonel Rodney Macklem, a.k.a. Baron Richard Torville, to seize the entire Louisiana Purchase, which figures also in *The Ferguson Rifle.* Villain needs heroine because of her deceased father's network of mercantile spies. Heroine could use the strength and resourcefulness of hero Talon but instead acts toward him with superciliousness because he is a shipbuilder, that is, a mere laborer. Oh, narrator Jean Talon is strong, all right; he confides in us that "[t]he bulges of my deltoids were like melons" (p. 37). He is shrewd too, sensing that Tabitha Majoribanks—that is the heroine's peculiar name—should be just about right to help him generate a mighty brood. There is detailed commentary about earlier Talons, all of which whets reader curiosity.

It could be shown that elements in this novel might challenge Jungian critics. After all, here we have young hero leaving homeland for adventure, semitemptress heroine (plus toothsome Yvette LeBrun, daughter of a Mississippi River keelboatman), and not one older male helper figure but two (piratical Jambe-de-Bois, who has a wooden leg; and Chateau, St. Louis merchant and source of news and aid). But I would rather note simply that the main attraction of this episodic narrative lies in its hints as to future accounts of earlier Talons.

Over on the Dry Side hangs in time awkwardly between the early action of *The Ferguson Rifle,* at one end of the timetable, and both *Borden Chantry* and *North to the Rails* at the other. But the relationship of Owen Chantry and other Chantry family members is not yet specified. Nor will *Fair Blows the Wind,* published still later but introducing family-progenitor Tatton Chantry (just as *Sackett's Land* introduced Barnabas late), help a whit. L'Amour specializes in confusing and thus teasing his loyal fans.

The primary narrator of *Over on the Dry Side* is teen-aged Doby Kernohan, who with his lonely Pa finds dead Clive Chantry. They bury him, take over his ranch and land as squatters, but then welcome Clive's scholarly brother Owen, who is also—quite awkwardly—a part-time narrator. Owen lets the two Kernohans stay as tenants working on shares, soon proves himself to be adept not only in storytelling scholarship (like Ronan Chantry earlier) but also both as a fighter and as a male attractive to a foxy female neighbor. This upsets young Doby, to our amusement. The girl turns out to be the stepdaughter of the leader of assorted thugs, all swarming about because rumor has it that Clive brought back a valuable treasure from Mexico. Thinking it gold, they can never believe that a historical manuscript could be worth more than tangible riches. A fine literary feature here is the use of Alfred, Lord Tennyson's majestic "Ulysses," one of L'Amour's abidingly favorite works, as source of clues leading to the treasure.

An interesting element of the narrative is the steady peeling away of members of the thug gang, until only an evil hard core remains. An incredible element is that eight named and also a few unnamed bad people get killed, whereas no good person dies. The main value of this complex novel lies in the characterization of Owen Chantry, a latter-day Renaissance man; again, his hints as to his illustrious family will help L'Amour keep customers buying his family serials.

Two Winners between Two Losers

Next come *Where the Long Grass Blows* (1976), *Borden Chantry* (1977), *Fair Blows the Wind* (1978), and *The Mountain Valley War* (1978). They seem not to have been written in this order, since the first and last are only competent, whereas the middle two are genuinely skillful.

Where the Long Grass Blows tells of yet another cowboy entering a strange region to stake his claim. He is callously willing to let rivals kill each other off, so that he can then solidify his holdings. But a villain wishes not only to do the same but also to capture the heroine by blackmailing her irresolute brother; so the hero takes sides. Not recommended.

On the other hand, *Borden Chantry* is a delightful Western detective story. Here L'Amour combines his knowledge of Western life and his unforgotten ability as a whilom writer of hard-boiled detective short stories. The titular hero is a wiped-out cattleman turned eastern-Colorado town marshal. The reader is thrilled to learn (at exactly the half-way point of the book) that the murder which Borden must solve is that of Joe Sackett, whom L'Amour mentioned in *The Daybreakers*, back in 1960, and never again until now. Borden assembles his evidence and tracks the killer. L'Amour increases reader anxiety by having Tyrel Sackett gallop in, urge Borden to get cracking, and threaten to take over if he cannot. L'Amour also makes Borden endearing through his modesty and poignant because his wife Bess (named Helen in *North to the Rails*), though loyal enough, cannot stand the snow and dust of the West, and wants to go back to Vermont with their son Tom (hero of the earlier-published *North to the Rails*). Nor does Bess cotton to the idea of her husband's interviewing local prostitutes to get vital evidence. We may wonder why anyone with magnificent Chantry blood coursing in his veins should wish to remain in this locale. But when Borden follows the killer into magnificent scenery, we have part of our answer. Highly recommended.[3]

L'Amour must have labored hard on *Fair Blows the Wind*. At 280 pages, it is one of his biggest novels to its date. The fact that it has seventy named characters, not counting a dozen or more historical personages glanced at, makes it a L'Amour block-buster almost on a par with the later *Bendigo Shafter, Comstock Lode, The Lonesome Gods*, and *The Walking Drum*. Its geographical spread is also extensive—more than that of *Comstock Lode* and *The Lonesome Gods*, but less than that of *The Walking Drum*.

Fair Blows the Wind follows its hero from the west coast of England into northern Scotland, then to London and the Channel region, and so to the Azores and Spain and the Lowlands, then back to London and to the Carolinas and finally to coastal Ireland. L'Amour is shadowy with his dates: he gives several but without permitting us to pin down the action on a timetable. I should say that the main events occur about 1573–90. The narrative sets and keeps a breathless pace but is weakened by one glaring fault: poor use of flashbacks. The first six chapters tell us about hero Tatton Chantry, marooned on a Carolina beach. Then we have a two-chapter flashback telling of his childhood. So far, exciting. But then we are barely in the present again when L'Amour takes us on a nineteen-chapter flashback, during which the stories are more exciting than Tatton's present, even when he falls in love on the beach. *Fair Blows the Wind* is still a swashbuckling romp of great verve and suspense. It also has a hundred hints that are all bits of the jigsaw puzzle ultimately destined to reveal the Chantry saga. Even as we read this installment we are witness to an ongoing myth-making process. Highly recommended.

The last novel of the Kilkenny mini-series to be published is *The Mountain Valley War*. In toto, the three seem disappointing. Perhaps L'Amour agrees, since Kilkenny has been shelved for the last several years. *The Mountain Valley War* offers little that is new. In it Kilkenny rides into southwestern Idaho to rest up, homestead, and build for a future that—like Jack Schaefer's hero Shane of *Shane*—may never be secure. Here, Kilkenny must again put his shining weapons at the service of justice. He cares for gun-orphaned kids, organizes good nesters, boxes a thug in town to attract legislative attention to the region's problems, and so on. Let us hope that even now Kilkenny, a.k.a. Trent and Lance, is enjoying his twilight years with ever-faithful Nita. To be avoided.

Two Block-Busters, Two Minor Works, and Two Sacketts

Next in order are *Bendigo Shafter* (1979), *The Proving Trail* (1979), *The Iron Marshal* (1979), *The Warrior's Path* (1980), *Lonely on the Mountain* (1980), and *Comstock Lode* (1981). The first and last of these, both monumental, show L'Amour's now persistent desire to break out of the old Western mold. *The Proving Trail* and *The Iron Marshal* offer nothing new. And *The Warrior's Path* and *Lonely on the Mountain* continue, out of chronological order, the saga of the Sacketts. The first concerns dead Barnabas's sons Kin and Yance; the second, Tell and his endangered cousin Logan Sackett up in Canada.

Bendigo Shafter should become a classic Western novel. It is a major work and a first-rate piece of fiction—clearly one of the four or five most important books thus far in L'Amour's career. Totaling 324 pages and divided into three numbered parts, it is longer with its forty-seven chapters than any of L'Amour's other big books except the later *Comstock Lode, The Lonesome Gods,* and *The Walking Drum*. Further, it is more shapely than any of them.

French-Canadian Bendigo Shafter narrates the story of his own maturing to responsible trail boss, town marshal, writer, New York visitor, and hunter and peacemaker among Indians. And all this from humble beginnings as teenaged homesteader (beginning about 1862) in the South Pass region of Wyoming, with his unhappily married brother Cain and family, with widowed young Ruth Macken and son, and with a number of other town-building pioneers. This community of hardy souls runs the moral gamut from benignant to depraved, especially when later increased by newcomers. It also boasts a pleasing variety of ages, from little kids to nubile girls to stalwart adults and on to one person trying for patriarchal status. Nor does L'Amour neglect Indians good and bad, white holyrollers, claimjumpers, and renegades. In all, his dramatis personae number more than eighty. Disasters natural and man-induced are numerous, but the men and women who surrender to the beauty and power of nature win out in the end. We have awesome challenges—blizzards, hostile or at least sullen Indians, distressed persons needing rescue, building problems, a cattle drive from Oregon, gold and the wingless vultures it attracts, would-be rustlers and other toughs, democracy vs. a kind of Plymouth Colony leadership system, a mountain lion, train-stalling buffalo, and even New York City roughnecks.

In spite of all that, we have surprisingly little violence and killing. One scene, reminiscent of John Steinbeck's *Of Mice and Men,* is climaxed when Ben's strong brother stops a would-be gunman by seizing his hand and crushing it. Western Ben prevents injury to himself in the East—specifically in New York City—by slugging one hired tough, getting the drop on his two unsavory associates, and then ordering them at gunpoint to beat each other up, all under the approving eye of an Irish policeman.

Bendigo Shafter has three rather equal parts. The first part (chapters 1–14) ends at the same time as Ben's youth. In the second part (chapters 15–35), Ben goes to Oregon for cattle and enlists the aid of Uruwishi, "the Old One," an ancient Indian warrior emeritus and easily the finest person in the novel. In the third part (chapters 36–47), Ben resists the temptations of New York, returns to the pioneering town in the South Pass region, but finds it half in decay, and heads with Uruwishi for the cleansing air of the sacred Indian Medicine Wheel in the Big Horn Mountains of Wyoming.[4]

With *Bendigo Shafter* L'Amour may be signaling his intention to characterize women with greater care. His nineteen named females here vary from Ruth Macken, perhaps suggested by early real-life Wyoming women politicians, to plain old loyal homesteading wives, to the beautiful child-woman Ninon Vauvert. Ben is smitten by Ninon's charms, and she precociously announces her amorous loyalty to him. L'Amour enjoys sending such girls out of the action for a while; in this case, Ninon goes on to New Orleans and elsewhere to continue her acting career. Typically open-ended, *Bendigo Shafter* concludes with more questions than answers as to her future with Ben—along with eight or ten unanswered queries floating in the reader's mind about other characters as well.

L'Amour flirts here again with an odd element frequent in romantic historical reconstructions. He has Ethan Sackett (who will later be named the uncle of heroine Echo Sackett in *Ride the River*) allow as how he had known John Colter, legendary Yellowstone explorer for a decade or so before his death way back in 1813. Another character, a reformed alcoholic gambler who takes up schoolteaching, says that he knew Edgar Allan Poe back in Philadelphia.[5] Hero Ben meets Horace Greeley in New York. And, best of all, old Uruwishi remembers Lewis and Clark.

The Proving Trail is a disturbing narrative of yet another teenaged cowboy whose vacillating father's murder shoves the lad into many adventures: abortive revenge, escape from ill-motivated relatives seeking his mystery-shrouded inheritance back east, contact with a pair of waitresses quite unlike in reliability, and a nightmare sequence of episodic pursuits and flights and fights. I am ashamed to confess that reading this work is exciting, because upon review it must be branded as almost totally ridiculous. It has a dozen authorial slips: a girl's aunt becomes her mother, a villain's wrist is broken but then evidently is not, the hero presciently analyzes a quasivillain without evidence, an older brother drops four years in age, suppositions become facts with unerring certitude, a map stitched into a jacket materializes in a buckskin container, the hero vows not to talk then talks aplenty, a girl's grandfather is reported with total gratuitousness to have known Sir Walter Scott, the hero vows not to shoot first then does so from ambush, three pursuers become four, and Huajatolla once named is then spelled Wah-to-ya. Worst perhaps, the hero suddenly decides not to hate his father's killer after all, deducing instead that everything is kind of inevitable. The best if most eldritch touch is L'Amour's introduction here of Haitian voodooism. *The Proving Trail* mainly proves that even a best-selling novelist can lose his artistic way now and then.

With *The Iron Marshal* L'Amour recovers rather nicely. It is a Western detective story, like *The Man Called Noon, Borden Chantry,* and *The Man from Skibbereen*, especially the last named, since the two works both feature Irish-born lads. The plot here is impossibly complicated and anticipates *Milo Talon* in its tangles. *The Iron Marshal* is unique for L'Amour: its two-chapter opening is cast in squalid lower Manhattan. After that, fleeing from a charge of murder (albeit justifiable), young hero Tom Shanaghy finds himself on a westbound railroad train (much like Cris Mayo of *The Man from Skibbereen*), from which he alights to danger (like the heroes of *Flint* and *Hanging Woman Creek*). Soon he saves a man from being lynched (as did the titular hero in *Utah Blaine*). By improbable subterfuge and with improbable rapidity Tom becomes marshal of a lawless Kansas town. Then, like the hero of *Borden Chantry,* he pieces together evidence, including not only items pointing suspiciously at a woman but also jottings in a dead man's notebook, to solve L'Amour's most complex plot puzzle yet, a suspenseful triple-cross.

Comstock Lode, just like *Bendigo Shafter,* is a block-buster and is clearly one of L'Amour's most ambitious efforts to date. In both, and in *The Lonesome Gods* and *The Walking Drum* as well, the author seeks to inject a degree of maturity in his heroes often absent earlier. The hero of *Comstock Lode* is Val Trevallion, born in Cornwall, son of migrating parents who are murdered on their way with him from Westport, Missouri, to the Far West for a life better than the tin mines of Cornwall can provide. Portuguese gold coins found submerged in the ocean off Cornwall financed the little family's venture. That same gold lured the depraved murderer and his nondescript gang to attack them in Missouri. Later it will be yet more gold—the gold, and also the silver, of the fabulous Comstock Lode starting in June 1859—that will beckon L'Amour's cast of dozens, good and bad, to western Nevada.

L'Amour skillfully prepares Val. He mined briefly for tin in Redruth, Cornwall, in 1849, when he was about thirteen years old. Then he traveled to New Orleans and Westport and attained orphan status in Nevada. Ten years pass (too blankly). Val, still eaten by a desire for revenge that he only partly sated, has arrived at glorious manhood, is versatile through having held a variety of catch-as-catch-can jobs during his awkward teen years and a little beyond, and leaves the Sierras for Virginia City and the Lode.

Precisely—too precisely—as in *Bendigo Shafter,* there is a traveling actress in *Comstock Lode.* She is the oddly named Grita Redaway, orphaned also during the attack in Westport but soon disappearing from Val's life, though never from his memory for her youthful sweetness. As with Ben Shafter's love Ninon, so with Grita: she is taken far away, becomes a brilliant actress, and returns like a happy fate to her never-lost love. Grita's career in San Francisco theaters inspires some of L'Amour's finest local-color effects. But the young lady must go on tour to the Comstock Lode region to be reunited with Val. In the process, she attracts the attention of the master villain, just as Val—like a few other L'Amour heroes—begins to fight the poisonous desire to continue with acts of revenge. Then it sadly becomes Val's fate to be unable to avoid the consequences in his own psyche of the evil that the murder gang inflicted—this because its leader and remnants are fated to attack Val before he can attack them. Thus the master villain becomes a kind of Faulknerian Flem Snopes, whom he also resembles in a few other ways as well.

L'Amour has effectively striven for variety here—in locales, kinds of labor, types of women, and degrees of unsavoriness among the thugs. One weakness: the incredible intrusion of coincidence. Val only quasi-reasonably returns to the place where his father died, in Nevada. Grita follows New Orleans and even faraway Paris with California gigs and then the Lode. Minor characters knowing one main character each are shoved by chance into the purview of another main character. In the entire vast West, where do the sought-for orphan-makers filter back to? Virginia City, of course. Why do they not change their names and avoid their nemesis? L'Amour would say that it is because he has written a latter-day Greek tragedy. Perhaps he has. *Comstock Lode* is a noteworthy achievement.[6]

A Trio of Mixed Voices

Milo Talon (1981), *The Shadow Riders* (1982), and *The Cherokee Trail* (1982), three totally different offerings, came next.

Milo Talon seems like a temporarily absorbing Western detective novel, sure enough; but no one should have to read it who has already perused such earlier L'Amour books as *The Man Called Noon, The Man from Skibbereen, Borden Chantry,* and *The Iron Marshal.* That is, L'Amour simply reshapes old plot effects into *Milo Talon.* Further, to attract continued reader interest he seems to figure that he must throw into his plot pot still more weird and improbable ingredients. Thus, in *Milo Talon* we have a uniquely odd situation. Let me try to put it all into one grotesque sentence with numbers used in place of characters' names, so as not to give away the plot. Milo is hired by evil Character No. 1 to find his "granddaughter" (No. 2), whose alleged inheritance he covets but who is really No. 3, and is the daughter of a strange man (No. 4—not No. 1's son No. 5) and a woman (No. 6) who later married No. 7, a decent business rival of evil No. 1, but left him to wed No. 1's no-good son (No. 5), whose father (No. 1) it becomes hero Milo Talon's aim to thwart through kindled love for No. 8, whose mother (No. 9) kept house for deserted No. 7 so nicely that he willed her daughter (No. 8) a fortune, which—you now see—is the object of ill-advised No. 1's greed but which "granddaughter" (No. 2?—no, really No. 3) never inherited at all. Very silly.

Milo Talon is going to be related in ways not yet delineated to muscular Jean Talon of *Rivers West.* We also know from *Ride the Dark Trail* and *The Man from the Broken Hills* that Milo is the son of Emily Sackett

Talon, whose ranch figures in the background of *Milo Talon,* since elusive No. 2 (really No. 3) stayed at the old ranch some time back.

Although in most ways *Milo Talon* is L'Amour's most needlessly perplexing novel to date, it does have a continually exciting sense of mystery, dispelled ineptly at times but still chilling. Further, there is poetic justice in the way villainess collides with female sadist toward the macabre end—also chilling in the extreme.

Now we hit *The Cherokee Trail,* which is different and very good. It echoes earlier L'Amour novels but is basically an original. Heroine Mary Breyton sneakily grabs the job of running a Western stagecoach station in northern Colorado when her Union army officer husband is invalided out in the middle of the Civil War and then is killed heading west to take that job. Her situation is thus the reverse of widowers in *Brionne, The Man Called Noon,* and *The Ferguson Rifle.* Resourceful though Mary is, she must occasionally summon a good man to help out, as in *Conagher.* Still, the way her ex-soldier father brought up the tomboyish girl at their estate called Harlequin Oaks in Virginia prepares her excellently to be self-reliant, Western style. In this respect she resembles do-it-yourself Scott Hardy of *Down the Long Hills.*

At its healthy core, *The Cherokee Trail* is new and fresh. It is, in fact, a dramatization of successful minorities in Western action: Mrs. Breyton is a widow in the West who declines to run back to her Eastern home. She has a little daughter, Peg by name, rather than a son—which might have been expected from the author of *Hondo, Brionne, Borden Chantry, The Quick and the Dead, The Walking Drum,* and so on. In addition, Mary and Peg are abetted loyally by Matty Maginnis, an Irish girl who decides to disembark from the stagecoach with Mary at Cherokee Station instead of going beyond. For balance L'Amour throws in two snooty daughters of a rich rancher not so far distant but that Mary can gallop over to borrow horses when need arises. Another minority is little Wat Turner, whose outlaw father has been killed by a local gunman and who turns up at the station. At first the kid is reluctant to accept aid from a woman; but before long he is cooperatively doing chores for his keep, flirting shyly with Peg, and listening to long fireside readings out of Sir Walter Scott. Even the Indians hereabouts are minorities. They watch, threaten a little, admire Mary's bravery, devour her cookies, and pay with antelope meat.

Mary Breyton is one of L'Amour's most engaging heroines. She works hard, sets a perfect example, demands and deserves respect, takes up weapons and uses them when she must, remains sweetly optimistic, lectures interminably, and thrills sympathetic readers with the poignancy of her recollections of the good old days in Virginia. Further, being feminine as well as competent in a man's job, she attracts a variety of males—attentive, flattering, watchful, doubtful, and of course downright vicious. The open-endedness of the last chapter leads me to suggest that L'Amour ought to write a sequel in which young Mary Breyton meets an unattached and gamey male Sackett.[7]

L'Amour at Last

The latest L'Amour titles are *The Shadow Riders* (1982), *The Lonesome Gods* (1983), *Ride the River* (1983), *Son of a Wanted Man* (1984), and *The Walking Drum* (1984). One of these is yet another Sackett segment. It is *Ride the River,* which stars Echo Sackett, a sixteen-year-old Tennessee girl (destined to fill out and become the aunt of Tell et al.) who journeys to Philadelphia in 1840 to claim an inheritance from the estate of Kin Ring Sackett and then get it back home again.[8] Another of these latest works is among L'Amour's most hasty and least effective efforts. It is *Son of a Wanted Man.* Two are epic efforts, one of which—*The Lonesome Gods*—builds on several previous books but is notable for new beauty and deeper wisdom, while the other—*The Walking Drum*—is unique for being cast in medieval Europe and the Near East.

The Shadow Riders seems to me to be in reality yet another Sackett with the names of the main characters changed. We have a Southern Ma and Pa, their three tough Southern sons, a couple of pretty girls, and well-armed foes. Mac Traven could easily be Tell Sackett, while his brothers Dal and Jesse Traven are clones of Orrin and Tyrel Sackett.[9] Once again, L'Amour avoids taking his hero through the Civil War, just as, to date, we know too little about Tell Sackett and the Civil War, but instead has Union army Major Mac Traven returning home at war's end to Texas just in time to rescue his Confederate army brother Dal from a passel of renegade would-be lynchers.

The novel then concerns the ugly subject of white slavery (as does *The Warrior's Path*): once home again, Mac and Dal learn that their brother Jesse has been wounded and abducted by ne'er-do-wells who have grabbed their sister Gretchen, Dal's fiancée Kate, and several other attractive women for sale down near Victoria, Texas (the locale of much *Matagorda* action). All this lucrative crime takes place to support a mad Southern colonel's desire to continue fighting for what all recognize as the Lost Cause—the now-ended Civil War. What follows is exciting and vigorous, but almost never new for L'Amour readers. For example, we have a lovable little girl (as in *Down the Long Hills*), a butchered dog (*Hondo*), and a semiretired pirate (*Lando, The Sackett Brand*). To me the most memorable tiny touch in *The Shadow Riders* comes when a decent bartender in Refugio expresses the hope that he will never again see his crooked brother, long unheard from: he will not, because Mac has just killed him down on the beach.

The Lonesome Gods, which in a 1979 interview L'Amour said he had conceived twenty years before,[10] became a money-making best-seller when it appeared in hardcover in 1984. L'Amour's longest fiction to its date, it required painstaking research and composition. L'Amour moved slowly for a change. He studied the property-owning habits of the Cahuilla Indians, traveled Mojave and Colorado desert trails again, deepened his comprehension of ancient Indian markers there, and made the desert his story's hero.[11] Even better, the divine spirit hovering over the desert waits—sometimes in vain—to respond to those who revere it. We read, "Men need their gods, but did not the gods also need men?" (p. 309). As in much of L'Amour's best fiction, here again we have a young boy maturing painfully, becoming more aware, learning to love the best in life—physical prowess, the brooding land teeming with God's creatures, a good woman, male camaraderie, the wisdom hived in books. Uniquely well here, L'Amour praises solitude and silence, the sea, Oriental sensitivity, and patience. Who should not become patient in the face of the conclusion that at times "[m]an . . . may seem a fragment, a chance object, a bit of flotsam on the waves of time" (p. 342)?

The Lonesome Gods is generally splendid. Its sixty-one chapters divide into eight odd-sized and unnumbered parts, thus: (1) chapters 1–11, (2) chapters 12–17, (3) chapters 18–26, (4) chapters 27–35, (5) chapters 36–41, (6) chapters 42–47, (7) chapters 48–59, and (8) chapters 60–61. (1) The young hero Johannes Verne (born in 1836) and his death-marked father escape into a desert sanctuary; (2) Johannes survives a murderous attack, gets through the desert to little Los Angeles; (3) a magnificent young woman, Miss Nesselrode, provides education and also protection for the boy, especially from his vicious Hispanic blueblood maternal grandfather, Don Isidro; (4) now mature, Johannes gathers wild horses in the desert; (5) he learns to fight, also falls in love; (6) he and his staunch friends pursue villains who steal his horse herd; (7) Johannes is alone in the almost pitiless desert, but has friends, wins out at last; (8) coda. It is impossible to summarize this complex plot in meaningful detail. There are more than a hundred major and minor characters. As usual, L'Amour has grave problems with his jumpy narrative points of view; he seems almost to make a virtue of his inability to create a single Jamesian "lucid reflector" for his action and philosophizing. Johannes tells his story in all or parts of some fifty-two chapters; but other narrators are enlisted to shed their light, especially Miss Nesselrode, and also both Johannes's dramatically unreliable girlfriend Meghan Laurel and Don Isidro, whom L'Amour sketches in grand bold strokes.

Is L'Amour reaching for bizarre character combinations here? The book includes a proud Spaniard who disowns his daughter, seeks to kill his son-in-law and then his small grandson, abandons a son because of his pathetic gigantism, and finds himself outmaneuvered by a weird but canny spinster sister. Further, the heroine, if Miss Nesselrode may be so denominated, brings to California an unnecessarily bewildering family background, an almost hypnotic ability to persuade others—especially inimical men and others whom she enlists to aid her pet Johannes—and also commercial savvy, which L'Amour often painfully explains to us was more common in Western women than standard history books admit.

When character and plot details fade, what remains in the reader's mind after a long encounter with *The Lonesome Gods*? Several things. The gods themselves, surely—sad but patient, in the desert heat waves and the cold mountain caves. A silent old Indian with a triangular blue stone suspended around his neck, who magically turns up to aid Johannes from time to time. A wild black stallion that seems to want the hero's friendship. But most of all that family-abandoned giant—tender, wise, stoical Alfredo—knowing that death is near for him and therefore seeking out an enormous stone seat high in the mountains where he can quietly watch the free eagles soar above him. To my mind, this scene is the finest that L'Amour has ever written. A rare rhetorical flourish in *The Lonesome Gods* is the hero's refrain "I am Johannes Verne, and I am not afraid," which the lad repeats both when he is plenty scared and after he proves his courage.[12] The refrain helps L'Amour create a fairy-tale atmosphere in the novel, which contains an evil grandfather, a patiently grinning murderer, a witchlike maiden great-aunt, a ghostly Indian visitor, a friendly horse, mysterious footprints, and a giant. Does modern realistic fiction need anything more?

Son of a Wanted Man is an embarrassment that never should have been published. It is a grievous example of L'Amour's hasty work between more artistic efforts. I would be tempted to regard it as ghost-written by a neophyte but for the fact that its style bears certain unmistakable L'Amour trademarks.[13]

The donnée of *Son of a Wanted Man* is exciting: what kind of loyalty does an innocent young fellow owe to an outlaw who has raised him thoughtfully? L'Amour had touched earlier on variations of this theme, in *To Tame a Land, Flint, Dark Canyon,* and *Reilly's Luck.* But here we have a practicing though over-the-hill Western criminal calling for his technically spotless foster son to join him in robbery. So far, a fine novel. But what happens is sloppily unfolded. Mike Bastian, aged twenty-two, has been trained by lectures, mapwork, and dry runs along the owlhoot trail to track, fight, and shoot. Then, though never tested in dust, rain, and blood, he is asked to take over the leadership of a gang of assorted toughs, who we are asked to believe have been waiting for him to come and order them back into bank- and train-robbing action. Nonsense. The heroine too has been kept in cellophane until the moment comes for her to meet the hero, who falls in love in about ten minutes. Nonsense again. These are two instances of unacceptable suspended narrative animation.

The most notable virtue of this potboiler is the reappearance of Borden Chantry and Tyrel Sackett, together again after their cooperative detective work back in *Borden Chantry.* In a curiously staged penultimate climax,[14] they help the young hero foil an elaborate robbery attempt, after which Borden, in law-and-order L'Amour's harshest paragraph, answers a young thug who has survived the gunplay, is arrested, and asks what is in store for him now. "Men who tried to steal the money others worked hard to earn got no sympathy from him [Borden Chantry]. 'For you? If you're lucky you may get no more than twenty years'" (p. 150).

The Walking Drum is a seafaring, overland-caravan, swashbuckling romp starring the boastful, attractive, impossibly versatile Mathurin Kerbouchard. He is the loyal son of a missing Brittany corsair and a murdered mother, and is bent on revenge and rescue and far-flung adventure. He is also a sailor, horseman, swordsman, archer, merchant, acrobat and juggler, magician and alchemist, storyteller, lover (manqué, I'd say), beggar, linguist (Arabic, Frankish, Greek, Hindi, Latin, Persian, Sanskrit), botanist, pharmacist, gourmet, physician, surgeon, demolition expert, and scholar (he can memorize and then "copy" books on chemistry, geography, history, literature, military art, music, philosophy, and religion). The time: 1176–80. And the place? Varied.

The action starts on the northwestern coast of Brittany, proceeds to Spain (Málaga, Cadiz, Córdoba, Zaragoza),[15] back to France then Flanders, then by merchant caravan east to distant Kiev, thence down to the Black Sea and Constantinople, Trebizond (Trabson), and finally southeast to Tabriz, Qazvin (Kazvin), and so to places better located on a map of *The Arabian Nights*—though near enough in soiled spirit to modern-day Tehran, Baghdad, and Basra. The main action is in Moorish Spain, benightedly Christian Paris and environs,[16] the brutal Russia of the Petchenegs (forerunners of Mongol tribesmen), Byzantine Constantinople, and the storied Selzuk Empire. Especially well evoked are Córdoba, Constantinople, and the Tabriz region. The helpful maps are the best thus far of those in any L'Amour book.[17]

The Walking Drum, the title of which comes from the cart-mounted drum pounded to set the caravan's pace, divides into an introductory chapter and then three fairly equal parts. The first part (chapters 2–23) concerns Kerbouchard's derring-do, amours, scholarship, and boastful antics in Spain. The second part (chapters 24–42) sees our hero join an enormous merchant caravan weaving its way from fair to fair in western Europe, then to Kiev, and encountering hideous disaster south thereof—on the shores of the Black Sea. Always Kerbouchard seeks his father; so the third part (chapters 43–57) takes our hero to Constantinople, to Tabriz and his perhaps ultimate love Princess Sundari Devi (from Anhilwara and heading back there in faraway Hind), and finally to the mountain fortress of Alamut in the Persian Valley of Assassins. And to his father? Read the novel.

The cast of characters is large, with almost eighty people directly involved in the bellicose, scholarly, amorous, picaresque activities of young Kerbouchard. A few—perhaps several, even—of these people are real: William [II] of Sicily (d. 1189); John of Seville (Johannes Hispalensus, fl. mid-twelfth century—Kerbouchard saves his life between Cadiz and Córdoba); Averröes (1126–98—Kerbouchard meets this important Spanish-Arabian philosopher-physician at a Córdoba party); Ibn-Beytar (ibn-al-Baytar, d. 1248—could he have actually been in that Córdoba coffeehouse for Kerbouchard to hear him discourse on botany more than seventy years before his death?); Abul Kasim Khalaf (abul-al-Qusim Khalaf, d. ?1013—perhaps Kerbouchard met his grandson); Ibn-Quzman (Arabian strophic, colloquial versifier-troubadour, d. 1160—sorry), Andronicus Comnenus (1110?–85), licentious cousin of Emperor Manuel I of Constantinople (Kerbouchard predicts in 1180 to Andronicus that the latter will become emperor

but be murdered by a mob [all true, in 1183 and 1185, respectively]);
Emperor Manuel I [Comnenus] of Constantinople (1120?–80)—Manuel in real life was both more passive and sicker in 1180 than
L'Amour's Kerbouchard notes); and finally Sinan (d. 1193), assassin
leader from Basra during the time of Muhammad II, 1166–1210 (L'A-
mour gives Sinan's full name as Rashid-Ad-din Sinan).[18]

Almost as important as real-life Arabs whom Kerbouchard meets are
the bewildering books he reads. A full list of named sources of his wit,
wisdom, historical and scientific and literary lore, esoterica, and trivia
would be ludicrously lengthy—as well as simply not to be believed. I
have no doubt whatever that neither Mathurin Kerbouchard nor Louis
L'Amour ever read with any degree of care one twentieth part of the
items named, which include in the space of five chapters alone (chapters 43–47) works of Aristophanes, Firdausi, Virgil, Homer, Pytheus,
Scylax, Eudoxus, Michael Psellus, Anna Comnena, Strabo, the Prince
of Gurgan, Sun Tzu, Procopius, Menander, and Xenophon. Earlier,
even more authors and titles—often Arabian—are offered, including
long-time L'Amour favorites al-Biruni,[19] Plutarch, and Vegetius, and
newcomers such as *The Ring of the Dove* and the rare *Ayennamagh*.

One set of books that L'Amour consulted and thoroughly used has
to do with costumes. A vivid feature of *The Walking Drum* is its careful
description of clothing, materials, and accompanying armament.[20]

Unlike all other L'Amour heroes thus far, Kerbouchard is a lover in
search not of a new home but an old father. So he loves at least the
following ravishing beauties with never a thought of settling down:
Aziza of Palermo (met at sea off Málaga), Sharaza (a brigand's daughter
in the mountains outside Córdoba), Valaba (a mysterious Córdoba host-
ess), Safia (Córdoba spy from Shiraz), Comtesse Suzanne de Malcrais
(met near Provins, outside Paris, and wanted for a political marriage
back in Saône, near Antioch), and incomparable princess Sundari Devi
(met at Tabriz, and wanted for an arranged marriage back in Anhilwara). There may be too much truth in Suzanne's taunting jibe at
Kerbouchard: "You have spoken so much of that [love-making] . . .
that I wonder if you are not just a talker" (p. 253). In sooth, *The
Walking Drum* contains more talk about lips, bosoms, thighs, hips,
intimacy, and sex than the rest of L'Amour combined. We even have
the word "fornication" (p. 312), mirabile dictu. The threat of castra-
tion also figures.

The story is graced by wild adventure told at a galloping pace. There
are a dozen grand climaxes. Splashy landscapes roll before our vision

through better wide-angle lenses than Hollywood could ever boast. But the work is marred by four things: the long arm of improbable coincidence, ill-digested background reading by its essentially unscholarly author, the besetting sin of heavy generalizations (some couched in elegant archaisms), and—inevitably, it now seems— wretched copyediting.[21]

Mat Kerbouchard is a survivor. I do not mind his multiple wounds. In an epic, we can expect the hero to be slashed in face, skull, thigh, to be slingshot across nose bridge, to be arrowed in side, to be cast on a fire for dead, to have a horse step on his foot, to lose a fingernail during a cliff climb. In truth, I can hardly wait to see Mat love and get wounded some more in the next two volumes of L'Amour's promised Middle Eastern medieval trilogy. So far, his hero is a captivating combination of cinematic figure, oneiric lover, and scholarly namedropper.

Chapter Six
The Family Sagas

To date, L'Amour has published seventeen novels concerning members of his Sackett family sprawling over three centuries and two continents, five novels about his Chantry family, and two about his Talons. He promises many more, especially about his popular Sackett lads. For example, he will narrate the life of founder Barnabas Sackett's strange son Jubal in the Far West shortly after 1630. Less firm would appear L'Amour's plan to cast Sacketts and Chantrys in an American Revolutionary War novel together. He will detail Tell Sackett's Civil War career and his first, hitherto-hidden love affair. L'Amour's Sacketts are supposed to intermarry with his Chantrys somewhere along the time line, probably late in the nineteenth century. The author has promised to explain about the shadowy progenitor of his Talons—a one-handed pirate, millionaire, and Gaspé settler in the sixteenth century.

Altogether, then, L'Amour has laid out ambitious plans for his family sagas. If carried to completion, books concerning Sacketts, Chantrys, and Talons may number about fifty.[1]

Literary Brethren

A number of writers have been as ambitious as L'Amour in writing family sagas, novels with reappearing characters, fiction that attempts to depict a historical epoch in a given region, and the like. Springing to mind at once are James Fenimore Cooper, Honoré de Balzac, Emile Zola, Anthony Trollope, John Galsworthy, Jules Romains, and William Faulkner. Also-rans include Thomas Hardy, who depicts an extended locale; Mark Twain, whose Tom Sawyer and Huckleberry Finn appear in several works (but never really grow much); William Dean Howells, whose Basil and Isabel March appear in eight fictional works; and Alex Haley, whose *Roots* traces families but makes one socio-political issue overridingly important.

L'Amour's story of Tell Sackett and his brothers, like Cooper's saga of Leatherstocking, is told out of chronological order but traces the characters as they move ever westward. Balzac was also influenced by

Cooper, and the development of his *Comédie Humaine* may have in turn influenced L'Amour with his family sagas. Balzac created over five hundred so-called *personnages reparaissants,* whose reappearances in various novels help unify his vast body of writings.[2] Further, he employed considerable so-called indeterminacy, which obliges the reader to exercise his imagination in filling gaps between the stories. Balzac also shifts his narrative point of view, presumably to help us see that big ideas must be studied from several angles. All of these devices are what one critic calls "means for evoking a sustained, almost obsessive interest in the reader."[3]

Zola, whom L'Amour has the hero of *Shalako* meet in Paris between wars and whom L'Amour also mentions in *Kilrone,* set an example for L'Amour by making his Rougon-Macquart novels a connected series. Zola followed Balzac's lead in using reappearing characters and unified his twenty books in the series by having them illustrate the transmission of hereditary traits through some thirty-odd family members in five generations. Parallels to L'Amour are readily noticeable. In addition, Zola had a relationship with his publisher as fine as that of L'Amour with his, if never so profitable for the earlier novelist: Zola promised a dozen novels (each longer than L'Amour's smaller paperbacks) in six years. Both men are exemplars of literary fecundity. The unity of L'Amour's family sagas is not precisely owing to any theory of heredity, but informing them all is surely the notion that the settlement of the Western frontier in America catalyzed saliently good and bad traits, that only the strongest survived, and that the Western movement illustrates a kind of Manifest Destiny. Further, most of L'Amour's Sacketts, Chantrys, and Talons are tall, strong males—perhaps a crude symbolism of the frontier's best genes in action. Three times we read in *Sackett's Land* about the dynastic pioneering destiny of the clan, while Tell Sackett later reports, "We Sacketts were healthy breeders, running long on tall boys. Counting ourselves, we had forty-nine brothers and cousins. Starting a feud with us didn't make any kind of sense. If we couldn't outshoot them we could outbreed them" (*Sackett,* p. 21). In The *Sackett Brand* he opines that he will "fight back" because "it was bred in the blood-line of those from whom I come, and I could not be other than I am" (p. 13).

We may turn to Trollope for the author among prolific novelists whose work habits L'Amour has most paralleled. In some 36 years Trollope produced 63 works in 129 volumes. How could he write so much? In his *Autobiography* he explains that he was at work each morning at 5:30, wrote 250 words per quarter hour by the watch in front of him, and easily produced ten book-size pages per day every day for ten months a year—or three fat novels per year normally. Moreover, he could compose anywhere—at home, at his club, aboard a train, or at sea.[4] Allowing for inevitable differences, we see a startling resemblance to L'Amour, particularly in Trollope's production of the interconnected Barsetshire Chronicles in six novels and the so-called Parliamentary Series (called *The Pallisers* on BBC television). The latter series, in addition, details the activities of some ten recurring characters—appearing not only in the main parliamentary novels but in six other works, including a pair of Barsetshire books.[5] This is surely analogous to L'Amour's habit of having Sacketts occasionally appear in non-Sackett novels.[6]

John Galsworthy and Jules Romains in our century resemble L'Amour too. Galsworthy once said that getting the idea on 28 July 1918 for *The Forsyte Saga* was the happiest day of his writing life.[7] Both Balzac and Zola had similar epiphanic moments during which they saw major phases of their lifework in a flash.[8] L'Amour can also recall the moment he was inspired to start the tale of the Sackett clan. In Tucumcari, New Mexico, he was getting the better of a fellow in a scrap when two of the loser's twenty-nine cousins—from two families—began to pitch in loyally. "So I began thinking about it [L'Amour reports] and I decided to write a story about a family like that, where whenever one of them was in trouble all the others always came to help."[9] As for *The Forsyte Saga,* it coalesced from 1906 through 1921, about as slowly as have the first seventeen volumes of L'Amour's Sackett saga. Then Galsworthy added five more works of fiction to make up *A Modern Comedy* (1929), and even wrote some Forsyte short stories three years after that. As Galsworthy notes, he was aiming at "the most sustained and considerable piece of fiction of our generation . . . [with] coherence and [power]," and "half a million words nearly. . . ."[10] L'Amour may be favorably compared to Galsworthy, since the former has thus far published close to a million words on his Sacketts. When we add in his Chantry and Talon novels, the total for potentially interlocking family sagas is far beyond Galsworthy's Forsyte word-count. Moreover, Galsworthy, like L'Amour, was motivated partly by a desire to show similarities between his own complex family tree and that of his fictional Forsyte family.[11] To a degree, L'Amour has done the same thing and may be counted on to do so substantially in the near future.

A twentieth-century author comparable to L'Amour in productivity and sweep is Jules Romains, although the latter has an obvious edge in profundity, historical grasp, and literary style. *Les hommes de bonne volonté* (1932–46) in twenty-seven volumes and about 2,500,000 words has twice the heft of L'Amour's three family serials to date. It has a more complex style and structure as well, but still it was aimed directly at the widest possible readership and tries to concern universal themes. Like L'Amour, Romains evokes a commonly understood national past to underscore the unity of his separate volumes. Like L'Amour, the French academician gives dates, mentions real-life events, and brings historical figures into the lives of his fictional ones—and all in the service of heightened verisimilitude. It is L'Amour's ambitious intent to do for three centuries of the American frontier what Romains has done for France in a crucial quarter of a century split by the years of World War I.

Comparisons between William Faulkner and L'Amour may seem grotesque. But, differences of substantive and stylistic elements apart, the two are alike in some respects. Faulkner vitalized a section of one part of America's Deep South, and populated centuries of it with family forebears and members of his Compson, MaCaslin, Sartoris, Snopes, Stevens, and Sutpen clans, among others of other colors. L'Amour vitalizes our South, Far West, and Northwest by depicting American Indians, whites, and Hispanics in friendship and strife over centuries as well. Both authors praise courage, endurance, the art of prevailing in the battle of good against evil, and the joy of worshiping the precious soil of the New World.

So it may be seen that L'Amour, like Balzac, uses reappearing characters, while like Zola he dramatizes families through successive generations. Like Trollope, he is an early-to-rise writing machine. Like Galsworthy he builds family sagas piecemeal but with an organic unity. Like Romains he combines fiction and history. And like Faulkner he shows various people worshiping a varied land but with interracial conflict staining it.

Sackettian Dramatis Personae

The Sackett books number seventeen through 1984. Perhaps about ten more will follow.[12] Just over fifty characters are Sacketts, including ancestors named and in-laws at least hinted at. Surrounding these Sacketts are some 732 other characters so far, including tangential historical figures—for verisimilitude and heightened action.

Narrator William Tell Sackett hints at the awesome spread and loyalty of his clan many times, notably as follows: "I've never seen more than a dozen [Sacketts] at one time except when great-grandpa and great-grandma had their wedding anniversary. There were more than a hundred men" (*Treasure Mountain,* p. 26). And Tell warns would-be assailants: "If they get me, there's fifty, maybe a hundred more Sacketts. They'll hear of it, and they will come ridin'. . . . [W]hen somebody kills a Sackett he buys grief and death and disaster" (*The Sackett Brand,* p. 99).

Not until his twelfth Sackett novel did L'Amour present the grand old patriarch of the clan, Barnabas Sackett, who is depicted back in the year 1599 as coming from the Welsh fenlands and wanting to "found a family . . . but not with a sword." Nor does he wish to stay in the undemocratic Old World; instead, he says ringingly of the New World, "This land was my destiny" and "This was the land!" (*Sackett's Land,* pp. 29, 76, 136). Oddly, after Barnabas and his marvelous wife, Abigail (daughter of an Elizabethan sea-captain), fulfill a prophecy voiced in *To the Far Blue Mountains* and have sons Kin Ring, Brian, Yance, and Jublain (Jubal), and daughter Noelle, Barnabas turns passive in Carolina: he lets Abigail, Brian, and Noelle return to London, then meets another prophecy by deliberately walking into an Indian trap, sword in hand and with flames leaping about him.

But never mind. The dynasty lives and spreads—already through Kin and Yance, perhaps later through Jubal when he emerges out in Colorado. Yance, wild and bushy-browed, roves as far as Massachusetts, gets into trouble there, and is put in the stocks. A fetching girl named Temperance (Penny) likes him, rescues him, and elopes with him—all in *To the Far Blue Mountains.*[13] Later Kin rescues Penny's Cape Ann friend Diana Macklin, a curiously modern and scholarly girl who has been snatched for the Jamaican white-slave trade. Kin follows the slapdash rescue with a moving marriage ceremony on a lonely Carolina beach, a ceremony conducted by a nautical minister whom old Barnabas saved in Newfoundland earlier and who married Kin's parents. (See *The Warrior's Path* and *To the Far Blue Mountains.*)

It is owing to Yance Sackett and his wife, Penny, that the Tennessee Sacketts so multiply. Tell Sackett reminds us a couple of centuries later that it was "ol' Yance . . . who founded the [Clinch Mountain] line way back in the 1600s" (*Lonely on the Mountain,* p. 14). But we still need details as to who founded the Sacketts from Cumberland, in Tennessee (i.e., Tell, Orrin, Tyrel, Bob, and Joe Sackett), and Denney's Gap (Flagan and Galloway Sackett). What about the forebears of Falcon and his son Orlando "Lando" Sackett (who hail from South Carolina, the Blue Ridge region, and Clinch's Creek), Parmalee Sackett (from Arizona and New Mexico), Emily Sackett (who through marriage to Reed Talon helps connect L'Amour's Sackett sequence with his Talon sequence), and Echo Sackett (from Tuckalucky Cove, Tennessee)? L'Amour in *Mojave Crossing* clarifies to a degree what continues to remain partly obscure when he has Tell say that "there were three kinds of Sacketts in Tennessee. The Smoky Mountain Sacketts, the Cumberland Gap Sacketts, and the Clinch Mountain Sacketts. These here last ones [Tell continues], they were a mean outfit and we had no truck with them unless at feuding time, when we were always pleased to have them on our side. . ." (p. 3–4).

Hints here and there permit us to conclude that Tell's generation of Sackett fighting males are mostly cousins. In *Treasure Mountain* we are twice informed that Lando Sackett is Tell's cousin. In *Mustang Man* narrator Nolan Sackett mentions "a cousin of mine . . . named Tyrel" (p. 35). In *The Man from the Broken Hills* narrator Milo Talon defines Civil War fighter Tell Sackett to the latter's admirers as "a cousin of mine. . . . My ma [he adds] was a Sackett" (p. 133).[14] In *Galloway* we read that Flagan and his brother Galloway Sackett are Tell's cousins too. And in *The Sackett Brand* shadowy Parmalee says that he is "from under the Highland Rim" (p. 127), while in *Galloway* he nicely insists that he and Galloway are not cousins; "Second cousins, I believe," he says (p. 149).

All this identification of Sackett cousins and second cousins helps little in sorting out their fathers. One exception is Lando's father Falcon. Though named and much discussed, Falcon Sackett is the most oneiric figure in the whole saga. Tell's father left his Tennessee family for the Colorado gold fields, where he died. Echo has some brothers, but only one is named. He is Ethan Sackett and becomes Bendigo Shafter's helper figure. Ethan explains that his father was killed by Comanches on the Sante Fe Trail when Ethan was only fourteen years old.[15] Another of Echo's brothers must become the father of Tell, Orrin, Tyrel, Bob, and Joe Sackett, since L'Amour tells us that Echo is their aunt.[16] Of the father of twins Logan and Nolan Sackett we learn nothing but that he loved the land and is now dead. The father of Flagan and Galloway Sackett, also deceased—like most fathers of dar-

ing young men in L'Amour's fiction—left Tennessee debts that his sons
return temporarily from the West to pay, in *The Sky-Liners*. Yance Sackett founded the Clinch Mountain Sacketts, and Logan and Nolan are
the Cumberland Gap brothers' cousins; so their fathers must have been
brothers, but L'Amour has not said so—yet. The Denney's Gap Sacketts are also cousins of these fellows; so their father must also have been
a brother of the fathers of Tell, Logan, Galloway, and their respec-
tive brothers. Galloway Sackett uniquely identifies Tyrel Sackett's
"pa . . . [as his] uncle" (*Galloway,* p. 36) and adds that the man was
in the Shalako region of southwestern Colorado at one time. Second-
cousin Parmalee Sackett's forebears line up shakily if at all, thus far.
And since Falcon Sackett married a Kurbishaw of South Carolina, he
may possibly have descended from Kin Ring Sackett, from way back;
young Echo Sackett, to be helpful, says that she has "kinfolk down to
Charleston" (*Ride the River,* p. 2) and thus may relate to Falcon in some
manner not yet specified.

For a writer who extols the deep joy of hearth and home, L'Amour
strangely depicts no Sackett heroes settling down much to such. Tell's
most poignant quest is for his father's grave far from home. Flagan and
Galloway have lost their Pa and return to pay his debts. Twins Logan
and Nolan have lost their father too, and even prefer as adults to remain
far apart; neither would appear ever to have been married. Falcon when
widowered left his son in selfish neighbors' incapable hands to go trea-
sure-hunting; later the two men queasily hanker for the same young
woman. Parmalee, one of my favorite Sacketts, is handsome and established, but mentions no family. And so on. Obviously L'Amour's purpose is to show male pioneers surging ever westward for adventure
before consummation of their dream of homemaking.[17]

Notice that the dozens of Sacketts not yet mentioned here, but about
to be briefly discussed now, show how skillfully L'Amour has played
variations on his major theme of adventure between home gone and
new home built. Ange Kerry is rescued by Tell Sackett in Colorado
(*Sackett*), is called his wife (*The Sackett Brand*), but is not seen again,
having been raped and murdered offstage. Echo Sackett's grandfather
Daubeny Sackett is described in *Ride the River* as having been a woods-
man, marksman, and log-cabin builder in Tennessee, also a Revolutionary War veteran and a deep reader. In *The Lonely Men,* published
earlier, we learn more about this man but without having his first
name. Drusilla Alvarado, a major Hispanic female character in
L'Amour (she is Mexican-Irish, like some characters in *The Californios*),

appears or is mentioned in eight novels. Tyrel Sackett meets her on her ancestral land in New Mexico, aids her sick grandfather (a splendidly evoked character), marries her, and takes her to Mora, where his career is then centered (*The Daybreakers*). Tell Sackett meets and admires her (*Sackett*); but, although she is often mentioned favorably later (even in non-Sackett *Catlow*), nothing is said about any children she and Tye have. Flagan and Galloway Sackett rescue Judith Costello from villains in Colorado (*The Sky-Liners*), and later stand off a different set of villains in the Shalako region, where Maighdlin Rossiter catches Flagan's eye (*Galloway*). But will either Judith or Meg become a motherly Sackett in due time? L'Amour stops short of ever saying so. Almost immediately after benighted Orrin Sackett weds narrow-eyed Laura Pritts, against the advice of cooler heads aplenty, she deserts him in favor of continued loyalty to her corrupt New England father. The only child Laura and Orrin have exists nowhere but in the vengeful mind of Laura, who sends Tell Sackett into Sonora after her nonexistent "Orry" in the hope that Apaches will kill him down there.

Minor Sacketts abound. Macon Sackett is a Clinch Mountain ginseng picker along the Ohio River, while Mordecai Sackett is a reclusive hunter, more a wailing wraith than that, but Echo Sackett's savior by the all-too-human means of homicide; both Macon and Mordecai appear in *Ride the River,* in which Echo calls the latter a kind of cousin. Uncle Regal, Echo's deceased father's tall brother, would also aid the girl on her Philadelphia mission but for a recent tussle with a bear that mauled him severely. Trulove Sackett, a gigantic Ohio River logger, would also come to her rescue but arrives with Macon, to whom he is vaguely related, only in time to tend the wounded and bury the dead. And Seth Sackett? Who is he? Named only once thus far (*Treasure Mountain,* p. 118), he may possibly be Tell's father, but we have no verifying evidence yet. Tarbil Sackett? When Emily Sackett Talon asks Logan if he is Tarbil's no-account Clinch Mountain son, the courteous gunman replies, "Grandson, ma'am" (*Ride the Dark Trail,* p. 24). Then there is Tell's grandfather who fought in the American Revolution, sailed with Captains Stephen Decatur and William Bainbridge, and battled Barbary pirates (*Sackett*): is this the same grandfather said by Tell in *Mojave Crossing* to have cut pirate Ben Mandrin's face in a swordfight off Hatteras? Flagan says in *Galloway* that his grandfather lived to be ninety-four years of age: he must have been a Sackett.

Of the 732 non-Sackett characters thus far in the Sackett series, a considerable number are *personnages reparaissants,* as Balzac would say.

For example, wily old Cap Rountree, loyal pal of Tell, Orrin, and Tyrel, appears in seven novels; the Tinker, named Cosmo Lengro once (in *Lando*), in six; Jublain (not to be confused with Jublain, nicknamed Jubal, Sackett), Barnabas's resourceful fighting ally, in three; and so on. In addition, we have, as in Romains, many historical figures who influence fictive plot situations. Examples abound and include Wyatt Earp and Bat Masterson, both rather important in *The Sky-Liners*; Governor Edmund J. Davis of Texas, offstage but significant (*Lando, Mustang Man*); Louis Riel and Alphonse Lepine (*Lonely on the Mountain*); and redoubtable Al Sieber (*The Sackett Brand*).[18]

Sack Time

The problem of dating events in the ongoing Sackett saga is sometimes perplexing. The seventeen volumes to date were published over a period of two dozen years and do not take up the action in chronological order. The novels thus far were published in the following order: *The Daybreakers, Sackett, Lando, Mojave Crossing, The Sackett Brand, Mustang Man, The Sky-Liners, The Lonely Men, Galloway, Ride the Dark Trail, Treasure Mountain, Sackett's Land, The Man from the Broken Hills, To the Far Blue Mountains, The Warrior's Path, Lonely on the Mountain,* and *Ride the River.* To make matters surely more trying for his own memory, L'Amour published forty-five non-Sackett novels while the seventeen Sackett works were appearing.

The Sackett books thus far fall into seven divisions: 1) *Sackett's Land, To the Far Blue Mountains,* and *The Warrior's Path* tell about Barnabas Sackett and two of his sons, Kin Ring and Yance—1599–1630; 2) *Ride the River* tells of two weeks in young Echo Sackett's life—1840; 3) *The Daybreakers, Lonely on the Mountain, Sackett, Mojave Crossing, The Sackett Brand, The Lonely Men,* and *Treasure Mountain* present a myriad of adventures in the lives of Tell, Orrin, and Tyrel Sackett—1866–78 (or a little later); 4) *Lando* concerns Orlando Sackett, and relates slightly to *The Sackett Brand* and *Treasure Mountain*—1867 (or 1868) –75; 5) *The Man from the Broken Hills* and *Ride the Dark Trail* are linked only because the narrator of the first, Milo Talon, is the son of Emily Sackett Talon, who is befriended by the narrator of the second, Logan Sackett; Logan also aided Tell of *The Sackett Brand* and later recalls having done so; 6) *The Sky-Liners* and *Galloway* feature adventures of Flagan and then his younger brother Galloway; moreover, in the earlier book Flagan remembers helping Tell of *The Sackett Brand*, while Flagan's Mexican friend Rodriguez recalls knowing a character portrayed in *The Daybreakers;* and 7) *Mustang Man* is narrated by Nolan Sackett, who is the twin brother of Logan and who meets a minor character figuring in events close to the end of *The Daybreakers.*

If the seventeen Sackett books through 1984 were to be listed in the order of their events, the group would contain only twelve titles whose relative positions are certain. They are *Sackett's Land, To the Far Blue Mountains, The Warrior's Path, Ride the River, The Daybreakers, Lando* (which starts after *The Daybreakers* but ends before *The Sackett Brand*), *Lonely on the Mountain, Sackett, Mojave Crossing, The Sackett Brand, The Lonely Men,* and *Treasure Mountain.* The other five are puzzling. *The Man from the Broken Hills* takes place before *Ride the Dark Trail,* which takes place after *The Sackett Brand;* but how much earlier is uncertain. *The Sky-Liners* occurs after *The Daybreakers* and *The Sackett Brand. Galloway* is enacted after *The Sky-Liners.* And *Mustang Man* comes shortly after *The Daybreakers.*

It seems regrettable that L'Amour did not preplan his saga of the nearly three-score Sackett people more carefully and write it all out with fewer interruptions. But for his own good reasons, when he was only about halfway through with the Sackett books to date he began two other ambitious family serials—those of the Chantrys and of the Talons. Detailed hints about these two families appear in four Sackett books to date. They are *Ride the Dark Trail, The Man from the Broken Hills, To the Far Blue Mountains,* and *Ride the River.* So it is clear that at least as long ago as 1972, the date of *Ride the Dark Trail* (Sackett No. 10), Chantrys and Talons were in the author's mind alongside his thus-far even more fertile Sackett clan. In fact, by then L'Amour had already published his first Chantry offering—which is *North to the Rails* (1971). In 1974, in his preface to *Sackett's Land,* he publicly announced his grand design:

Some time ago, I decided to tell the story of the American frontier through the eyes of three families—fictional families, but with true and factual experiences. The names I chose were Sackett, Chantry, and Talon. . . . Story by story, generation by generation, these families are moving westward. When the journeys are ended and the forty-odd [make that fifty?] are completed, the reader should have a fairly true sense of what happened on the American frontier. (pp. v–vi)

An author born in 1908 and making such a statement in 1974 was bold indeed. By that latter year, L'Amour had published twelve Sacketts, two Chantrys, and no Talons, or fourteen of a projected forty to fifty titles—that is, less than a third done in a writing career starting late and already spanning more than a quarter of a century. And, to boot, L'Amour has now published *The Walking Drum,* the first volume of his announced Kerbouchard trilogy.

Most of L'Amour's family-saga serials may be dated easily. Like Balzac, Zola, Galsworthy, Romains, and Faulkner, their author occasionally sprinkles dates at key points. Nevertheless, like Balzac and Faulkner, among others, L'Amour makes little mistakes or at least remains obscure.[19]

The Sackett subset featuring Barnabas Sackett and his sons Kin Ring and Yance is easy to date. *Sackett's Land* opens with the year stated to be 1599. *To the Far Blue Mountains* continues from 1600 to the Jamestown Massacre of 22 March 1622, and then perhaps a couple of years beyond. *The Warrior's Path* mentions the year 1630 early in the text. But then a curious hiatus follows until *Ride the River* resumes the action in the advanced year of 1840; in this novel Echo Sackett twice reminds us that Barnabas was clan founder.[20]

Next comes the subset of seven novels featuring Tell Sackett and his two most important brothers, Orrin and Tyrel. Only a few hints in these works sketch in bits of action from Kin's and Yance's time to that of Tell et al. In *Lonely on the Mountain* Tell recalls that "[i]t was old Yance Sackett who began it some two hundred years back"—"it" being the family stock-driving "way of life." A little later Tell explains that twins Logan and Nolan were "Clinch Mountain Sacketts, right down from ol' Yance" (pp. 5, 14). In *The Lonely Men* Tell reports this: "My great-grandfather fought in the [American] Revolution. He was with [Colonel Henry] Dearborn [a distant L'Amour relative (see *Frontier,* p. 66)] at Saratoga [1777], and he was in Dearborn's command when they marched with General [John] Sullivan to destroy the towns of the Iroquois [1779]" (p. 122). And in *Mojave Crossing* Tell reminds Ben Mandrin, as noted, that his grandfather had a sword fight with piratical Ben of Hatteras long before.

Now for a problem. Just when might William Tell Sackett have been born? When *The Daybreakers* opens, in 1866 (in *Treasure Mountain* Orrin explains that he and Tyrel "crossed the plains in '66 and '67" [p. 45]), Tyrel is eighteen years old, Orrin is twenty-four, and Tell is said to be the oldest brother. Next, Tell narrates all or most of *Sackett, Mojave Crossing, The Sackett Brand,* and *The Lonely Men.* Early in the first of these he says that he is twenty-eight and four chapters later identifies the year as 1875. But wait: from data in *The Daybreakers* we may infer that Tell is at least twenty-five in 1866, hence at least thirty-four, not twenty-eight, in 1875.

L'Amour places a bit of action in *Mojave Crossing* at Cahuenga Pass, outside Los Angeles, and says that the celebrated outlaw Tiburcio Vasquez was captured there a while back. His arrest occurred 4 May 1874. Better for dating purposes, L'Amour also says that Tell's beloved Ange Kerry (whom he rescued in *Sackett*) is visiting relatives back in the East. By the start of *The Sackett Brand* Tell calls Ange his wife and soon thereafter reports the exact date of her murder—25 April 1877. Local-color details add to the verisimilitude of L'Amour's plot here: the great Apache leader Victorio happens by, in the Mogollons, to tend Tell's wounds, in implicit praise of his bravery, and then sees Tell on his way to Camp Verde, where he encounters equally famed scout Al Sieber. Both Victorio and Sieber were in this region in 1877.

But with *The Lonely Men* we encounter a few more time problems. Since Tell informs his friends that Ange is dead, the time must be late 1877 or a little after that. Next, Orrin's unprincipled ex-wife Laura persuades Tell to risk his neck in an attempt to rescue her imaginary son. Admittedly, Tell has often been away from his brother Orrin, who married Laura in Mora in 1867 but left her soon thereafter because of her disloyalty. It must seem to most careful readers that Tell would have heard that Orrin is not the father of any child by Laura. Furthermore, back in *Sackett* Tell visited his aged mother in Mora, where she was living with Tyrel and his lovely wife Drusilla; mention would surely be made of Laura's defection to her criminal father's side. So L'Amour can hardly expect to wiggle off the hook when he lamely has Tell comment thus about Orrin in *The Lonely Men:* "I did recall some talk of his marrying, but none of the details" (p. 18). In addition, the action of *Lonely on the Mountain* takes place in 1870, at which time Tell and Orrin ride the range together for weeks; they would have discussed deceitful, depraved, and childless Laura.

Both *Lonely on the Mountain* and *Treasure Mountain* are bothersome as to datable action. The former reads as though it ought to be taking place much later than the time frame occupied by the novels from *Sackett* through *The Lonely Men*. Further, we learn in *Lonely on the Mountain* that Orrin reads a lot, including the *Century* magazine, which was founded in 1881. This date, for a late cattle drive by Sackett brothers gathering to aid their jeopardized cousin Logan, makes more sense[21] than the action's true date of 1870. This date must be correct, however,

because L'Amour vivifies the Sackett cattle drive northwest of the Dakotas and into Canada, then west of Forts Qu'Appelle, Carlton, and
Garry, south of Winnipeg, through having Orrin arrested by métis
leader Louis Riel's men at Fort Garry on the Canadian Red River.
L'Amour introduces Riel as the leader of an insurrectionary provisional
government established at Fort Garry after the Hudson's Bay Company
left Prince Rupert's Land and the métis justifiably feared that their way
of life would be submerged once whites flooded in from eastern Canada. In real life, Canada took control of the region on 1 December 1869,
by which time Riel had seized Fort Garry, executed a white Canadian
rebel against his National Committee of the Métis of Red River, then
had been unable to solidify his gains and sought amnesty, failing which
(on 24 August 1870) he escaped into the Dakotas. Since Riel gives
Orrin permission to drive his supply carts through, and since the cattle
drive continues later—through June and July, we read—the date of
action of *Lonely on the Mountain* must be 1870. [22]

The dating of *Treasure Mountain* is easy, but the novel includes a
temporal error. Since early in the story Tell reminds himself that his
wife Ange is gone and further that he doubts he will ever again see
Dorset Binney, heroine of *The Lonely Men,* the action of *Treasure Mountain* must follow that of *The Lonely Men,* which itself takes place after
The Sackett Brand, to be placed in 1877. Further, twice early in *Treasure
Mountain* we read that its action starts in the wild New Orleans of the
1870s. So let us call it 1878 or 1879. Now the problem. Tell and
Orrin in *Treasure Mountain* undertake the mission of finding the trail
of their father, long missing in the San Juan Mountains of Colorado;
they iterate monotonously that they are following a trail now twenty
years old. But back in *The Daybreakers* Ma Sackett reminisced (in 1866)
with her son Tyrel thus: "Eighteen years now I've seen you growing
up, Tyrel Sackett, and for twelve of them you've been drawing and
shooting. Pa told me when you was fifteen [i.e., in 1863] that he'd
never seen the like" (p. 3). So why does L'Amour repeatedly tell us in
Treasure Mountain that Pa Sackett has been missing for twenty years,
that is, since 1858 or so? The answer is that, like Balzac and Faulkner,
he was a little careless here.

Lando is easy to date, except for its start, which may be in late 1867
and certainly by 1868. Two dates are given. They are 1868 and 19
November 1875, the latter being the day Lando escapes from the Mexican prison in which he has been confined for six years. One wonders
what the significance is of that precise date, beyond the fact that the
prisoner would surely remember it well. *Lando* connects loosely with

two of the seven novels starring Tell, Orrin, and Tyrel. When Lando hears in *The Sackett Brand* that Tell is in deep trouble in the Mogollons (in 1877), he quits a winning poker game and rushes to his aid. Two Tell novels later, in *Treasure Mountain,* Tell at Webber's Falls secures fresh horses from a man who knew Lando shortly after he got out of prison and gratefully recalls betting on his pugilistic skills in Texas.

The Man from the Broken Hills is unique among the Sackett novels for the simple reason that it is not a Sackett novel at all, but a Talon novel, in spite of Bantam advertisements to the contrary. Its narrator is Milo Talon, and it connects with the real Sackett books only because *Ride the Dark Trail* is narrated by Logan Sackett and details his meeting with Milo's mother, Emily Sackett Talon. In *The Man from the Broken Hills* Milo recalls leaving the Colorado family home three years earlier and starting to ride the outlaw trail, "[n]ot [he adds] that I was an outlaw" (p. 6). Later he tells some cowboys, when they are discussing Union army soldier Tell Sackett's phenomenal marksmanship during the Civil War, that Tell is his cousin; he elects not to add, however, that Milo is a confederate army veteran, having joined at age seventeen and rising to the rank of lieutenant. This fact comes out not here but in *Ride the Dark Trail.* Questions arise. When did Milo leave home? Did he leave as a restless teenager, get caught up in Civil War service, and thereafter ride the outlaw trail? Or did he leave home to sample the owlhoot trail at once? Evidence in *Ride the Dark Trail* permits us to answer the first question in the affirmative, but evidence from *The Man from the Broken Hills* points toward a yes to the second question. Perhaps Milo and L'Amour, in the second novel at least, both forgot that Milo fought in the Civil War.

Since Logan, narrator of *Ride the Dark Trail,* recalls riding to help Tell from troubles recounted in *The Sackett Brand,* that is, in 1877, *Ride the Dark Trail* must occur still later in the 1870s. It is not of much help to the dating of either *The Man from the Broken Hills* or *Ride the Dark Trail* for L'Amour to refer to Brown's Hole, as he does in the former work, or when in the latter one he sends Logan up there to leave a message for Milo. Brown's Hole activities involving Isom Dart, Tip Gault, Mexican Joe Herrara, and at least one of the Hoy boys, all of whom Logan encounters, were simply too extensive in time—although, to be truthful, Logan close to 1880 might not really have found so many gunnies in the Hole as he fictively did.[23]

The Sky-Liners, Galloway, and *Mustang Man* are connected only tenuously to the other Sackett novels thus far. For example, in *The Sackett Brand* we read that when Tell is in trouble in the Mogollons (1877), his cousins Flagan and Galloway rush to help. These same brothers are the heroes of both *The Sky-Liners* and *Galloway*. L'Amour dates *The Sky-Liners* by one subtle historical aside: when Flagan and Galloway pass through Dodge City, they meet Marshal Wyatt Earp and Sheriff Bat Masterson. As Western history buffs can all attest, this places the action in the year 1878.[24]

Mustang Man connects least of all with other Sackett books. Late in the story its titular hero Nolan is befriended by Ollie Shaddock, who was the sheriff that advised young Tyrel Sackett to leave Tennessee and head west, since he had killed a Higgins during the Sackett-Higgins feud. Further, it was Ollie who had transported Ma Sackett and her youngsters out to Mora, where Ollie subsequently wished to enter local politics. But by the time of *Mustang Man* he is in the wagon-freighting business out of Santa Fe and fortuitously hires Nolan in the violent little town of Loma Parda. Early in the novel Nolan recalls hearing "from the Davis police" (p. 31). This would be a reference similar to one in *Lando* concerning Governor Edmund J. Davis, whose criminal, carpetbagging police made Texas hot for good men as well as bad in 1868, 1869, and 1870. So the action of *Mustang Man* might be 1875, or later by two or three years.

The Best of the Sacketts

For what it may be worth, I should like now to indicate my favorite Sacketts. The best-modulated quintet, in order of my preferences, is composed of *The Daybreakers, To the Far Blue Mountains, The Sackett Brand, Sackett's Land,* and *Ride the Dark Trail. Sackett's Land* starts it all, with old Barnabas leaving the socially stratified England of Queen Elizabeth and Shakespeare for the Carolinas, with their Indians and beaches, their opportunities for adventure and trade. *To the Far Blue Mountains* shows Barnabas prospering in family and money, and starting his dynasty, especially with Kin Ring and Yance, and perhaps Jubal too. *The Daybreakers* is an exciting novel in its own right, though flawed in the characterization of minor figures, and has the added advantage of first presenting Sackett brothers of post-Civil War times. *The Sackett Brand* continues the adventures of Tell, already known, and shows him in anguish and with hatred. *Ride the Dark Trail* begins to introduce us to a different breed of Sackett, in doughty owlhoot Logan, and also connects Sacketts to Talons through Emily Sackett Talon.

Most of the other Sackett volumes have their individual virtues, in greater or lesser degrees; but perhaps the following five are the least effective, least persuasively innovative: *The Lonely Men,* the plot of which is started up and powered only by a lie. *Mojave Crossing,* which sprawls and also has an unbelievable villainess. *Mustang Man,* more of the same, starring Logan's twin Nolan in a plot that does not hold together. *Treasure Mountain,* a Gothic crazy quilt, with villains too heavy to make their defeat believable, a missing diary found peacemeal, and a Sackett brother who quits on us. And *Ride the River,* which is merely another L'Amour hide-and-seek romp, though starring a feisty little female for variety.

What we take of substantive value from a study of L'Amour's Sackett volumes thus far is a memory of separate exciting adventure canvases, unrolling with their variegated backdrop of American frontier history, and stitched together by the sturdy Sackett (read "American") virtues of self-reliance, courage, stoicism, loyalty, and martial smarts. America is hooked: Americans will buy any number of additional Sackett books, even though many such works could reveal stories as gripping and artistic if the name Sackett appeared nowhere in them. All of which, if true, only goes to underline the hypnotic drawing power of the Balzacian *personnage reparaissant.*

Chantrys and Talons

It seems likely that L'Amour has bitten off, or rather spoken about, more than he can manage. He has, however, recently scaled down his plans slightly. In a September 1981 interview he said that he had traced his Sackett family back to the fifteenth century (as though they were real people), and planned ten more Sackett novels, at least five more Chantrys, and probably five more Talons (*Comstock Lode,* pp. [421–22]). By the time of that interview, L'Amour had published sixteen Sacketts, five Chantrys, and two Talons; I figure that he then was projecting about twenty-six Sacketts, ten Chantrys, and seven Talons in all, or forty-three or so titles altogether in his Sackett/Chantry/Talon supersaga. In a 1983 interview published by Bantam, L'Amour reiterated previous commentary and added new data concerning both the Talons and the Chantrys, thus:

The original ancestor of the Talons was a one-handed pirate [so indicated in *The Man from the Broken Hills, Milo Talon, Rivers West,* and *To the Far Blue*

Mountains], a very dangerous old man who came over here with many millions of dollars and settled in the Gaspé Peninsula in Canada. I haven't told much about him but he is one ancestor who lives on through the rest of his family. He's left his mark on all of them. The Talons become builders in the New World. Jean Talon, in *Rivers West,* for instance, is a man who builds with heavy timber. . . . He built bridges. He built churches. He built ships. He built steamboats. He built whatever there was to build. And he comes west at the time [1821] when they're building steamboats in Pittsburgh, which is the focus of my novel [not so].

Fair Blows the Wind is the story of Tatton Chantry. That isn't his real name. I never tell his real name and I never expect to tell. I'm the only one who knows. Even his wife [Guadalupe Romana Chantry] doesn't know. But he was a descendant of Irish kings. His father was killed by the British and he had to leave Ireland in a hurry, and he takes that name. He stows away in a ship thinking he's going to France and winds up in England. Then, through a series of adventures, and a lot of sword fighting, he comes over to America. He lands over here on the coast of Carolina.

The Chantrys and Talons are allied in different points in time by marriage with the Sacketts [only once to date: Emily Sackett wed Reed Talon]. And their lives run parallel, especially the Sacketts and Chantrys. Very early on, individuals of the two families meet and then part and then meet again [as in *Borden Chantry* and *Son of a Wanted Man*].[25]

Back in the 1981 interview L'Amour offered the following of interest by way of contrasting traits of his three main fictional families:

Yes, there is a relationship. The Talons are builders primarily. They hail from Brittany [like the Kerbouchards of *The Walking Drum*]. They are one way or another caught up with building. Milo Talon not so much [i.e., not at all], . . . but most of the Talons in the stories should be building, bridge construction, ships, that sort of thing. The Chantrys are better educated than the other two [families] and they're Irish and are involved in statecraft and many other things. The Sacketts are primarily frontiersmen. (*Comstock Lode,* p. [422])

Obviously, future Chantrys and future Talons will have to prove to be more scholarly and more constructive, respectively, than most of the ones we have encountered in the seven novels telling us about them to date. Just as obviously, few members of one family have met members of the other—so far.

In order of action taken up, the first seven Chantry/Talon volumes begin with *Fair Blows the Wind,* which tells us that the Irish father of hero Tatton Chantry was killed by the British in Ireland about 1573 or so. He left his son memories of a beautiful coastal home, scholar-ship, gems, and swordsmanship. Tatton, the narrator, adds that his deceased "mother's people were of the *Tuatha De Danann,* who ruled Ireland before the coming of the Milesians" (p. 51). Tatton takes the name Chantry from someone else. We read:

> Tatton Chantry . . . a borrowed name belonging to a man long dead, a man from where?
> Who had he been, that first Tatton Chantry, that stranger who died?
> I remembered him from my father's time, remembered the night we had lifted him from the sea, a handsome young man, scarcely more than a lad.
> Dead now . . . yet living in me, who bore his name. Had he family? Friends? Estates? Was he rich or poor? Brave or a coward? How had he come where we found him?
> A mystery then, and a mystery still. (p. 30)

I must confess that the mystery seems to me to have more than its proper share of Poesque fudge in it. Late in the story, all disasters behind him and much passion spent, Tatton and his wife Guadalupe have a son back in Ireland, about 1590. End of that story.

Next is *The Ferguson Rifle,* which discovers for us Ronan Chantry leaving North Carolina and then Boston for the West to hunt in the newly acquired lands of the Louisiana Purchase, about 1804. Now this leap through the centuries from the late sixteenth century to the early nineteenth bridges too much, in my opinion, for L'Amour ever to fill up with his promised five more Chantrys. Next in the Chantry/Talon saga comes *Rivers West,* which presents to us the earliest Talon thus far. He is Jean Talon, the muscular timber-wielder, who since he starts out in the novel from the Gaspé must be a direct descendant of rich, pirati-cal old Talon the Claw. Like Ronan, Jean too heads for the Louisiana Purchase; so once we meet scholarly Owen in *Over on the Dry Side* in western Colorado in 1866,[26] we are not surprised that the next Talon segment stars Milo, who in *Milo Talon* continues the adventurous life that began—for us—in *The Man from the Broken Hills.* It should be mentioned, although L'Amour himself has tried by his interview com-ments to spike this objection, that for a member of a building family Milo does little to honor his family tradition except, perhaps, to build a successful case against a scoundrel who hires him to do some detective work.

And then comes *Borden Chantry,* the titular hero of which, though a Chantry, is no scholar whatever. So, like Milo Talon, he is deviating from family tradition. Nor is his son Tom Chantry likely to be very learned with respect to books and such, since the family has been wiped out by adverse Colorado weather (in the early 1880s) and Borden, as we know, has become a law officer. Next chronologically is *North to the Rails,* which—having been published earlier and reporting that Borden was murdered—features young Tom Chantry, grown up in the softer (pro-Chantry?) East, but not scholarly in any sense, and now back in the West heading up a cattle drive perhaps as late as 1890. This date, however, could stand some clarifying by L'Amour.

Other Chantry action is minimal. In *Ride the River,* eighty-year-old Finian Chantry is a Philadelphia lawyer who aids Echo Sackett, not least by ordering his handsome, strong, spoiled nephew Dorian Chantry to help the girl once she starts heading west again. And in *Son of a Wanted Man* Borden Chantry joins law-and-order forces with Tyrel Sackett.

What can ambitious L'Amour do to fill ultrawide temporal gaps in his ongoing Chantry and Talon mini-epics? He offers one substantive hint that I know of. In that already-cited 1981 interview he says, "I've got a book planned set during the American Revolution in which I will have a Sackett on the frontier and a Chantry in the seats of the mighty, you might say" (*Comstock Lode,* p. [422]).

But we still need much action between, on the one hand, the early seventeenth century of Tatton Chantry in Ireland and Barnabas Sackett's sons Kin, Yance, and elusive Jubal in America, and, on the other hand, the beginning of revolutionary unrest in colonial America late in the eighteenth century. Could L'Amour conceivably plan to cast a book or two in the epoch of the French and Indian War, before the American Revolution? It is much to be doubted. Yet he has said that his vast sweep of fiction, when complete, will tell the story of the ever-advancing American frontier. In addition, he might be expected to treat the Civil War—perhaps only tangentially, as it impinges on the Southwestern frontier. He has promised a novel about Tell Sackett in the Civil War, and we know from earlier hints that Tell joined the Sixth Cavalry in Ohio, was captured at Shiloh, was exchanged, and then fought the Indians in the Dakotas.[27]

Before L'Amour issued his first Sackett/Chantry/Talon volume, which was *The Daybreakers* (1960), he had published seventeen novels. From 1960 through 1964, four of his fourteen novels (29%) were Sackett/Chantry/Talon books; 1965–69, four of fifteen (27%); 1970–74, six of fourteen (43%); 1975–79, six of twelve (50%); and 1980–84, four of ten (40%). Since starting his three-family serials, 37% of his novel production has concerned one or more of those families. Yet for ambitious L'Amour, there are also other, nonsaga works to write, Western and otherwise. If the above figures point to anything, they may mean that while he writes his nineteen or so still-projected family works, they will be but 37% or so of some fifty (or more) new works in all. Of them, some may be innovatively non-Western. Louis L'Amour has now begun his medieval European and Middle Eastern "frontier" Kerbouchard trilogy. And he has already staked a claim on that final frontier—mankind's Space.

Chapter Seven
Style and Message

The fiction of Louis L'Amour fulfills the first requirement of narrative literature: it is exciting. But it does not fulfill enough of the criteria of literary art. Although it reveals much about its author, holds up a mirror to an epoch, and teaches the reader something of abiding value, the age that it reflects is not L'Amour's but a bygone time, and his art though vivid is often flawed and cannot be called organic.

L'Amour is a bestselling anachronism. He writes gripping melodrama, not tragedies. His heroes could be killed at any time, and this would end the adventure. But they always survive, as in happy-ending fairy tales. His heroes are often epic questers, possessing the virtues of Ulysses, but not those of Aeneas or Dante. They use all weapons that are at hand, including cunning, to win through to the establishment or reestablishment of a happy home, either for themselves or for others. Hence their future is not national so much as it is personal. Nor do L'Amour's characters learn much through suffering. They usually wind up, rather like Robert Frost, only more sure of all they thought was true. Still, they are melodramatically heroic figures, whereas, since his villains usually fail, fall, and never learn much, they are mostly absurdist characters.

L'Amour stresses the endangered American virtues of violent patriotism. He shows us the values of fighting for family, home, region, country, the frontier way of life. Hence he is more an entertainer than an epic spokesman for a nation, as he tends wrongly to define himself. His vast reading public finds him comfortable to like, because he is exciting and also reinforces our notion that the fading American way of life—nothing less than the dramatic destiny of a westering people— has been presented with justifiable pride.

"Just a Story-Teller"

"[D]on't put me down as a novelist, and don't say I'm an author. I'm just a story-teller, a guy with a seat by the campfire. And I want to share with people what I have found, and what I have seen, and the wonderful old voices of men and women talking of those bygone times."[1] So says L'Amour of himself. Further, he has said that he never plots a story in advance. "I always write off the top of my head, although the story locale and characters have often been in mind, or partly so, for some time."[2] Finally, he once boasted as follows: "I go over it [the first and only draft] to correct typos. No editor has ever given me advice or suggestions. They just ask when they will get the next book."[3]

These statements, though doubtless candid, provide L'Amour with an unconscious rationalization of certain stylistic faults. But first, on the more positive side, they highlight his main strength, that of an old-fashioned tribal historian. The most important thing for a tribe is its ground. L'Amour starts with that. Next come the heroes exploring and defending that ground. L'Amour always imbeds his best characters in their locale. He is a master of scenic description.

Living Nature

When I first read through L'Amour's complete fiction, I marked every painterly setting. Vivid ones are numerous beyond belief. L'Amour is a master at describing dawns, sleepy noonings, sunsets, deserts and canyons, volcanic and mountain scenes, shimmering summer, autumn foliage, winter blizzards and forest snow, and verdant spring again, seascapes and ocean storms, clouds, moonlight, and rain, and especially animals in glorious movement in their habitat.[4] Over and over again, he advises us to study a given scene in different lights. For example, in *Callaghen:* "One really never knew mountains unless he had seen them at both sunrise and sunset" (p. 31).

The temptation is to quote too extensively from this author for whom "[n]o amount of seeing ever made nature old to him" (*Over on the Dry Side,* p. 85). Sometimes the picture is general: "This was my world, this barren, lonely place, this vast pink-and-copper silence, this land of dancing heat waves and cruel ridges. Here where even the stones turned black from the sun. . ." (*The Lonesome Gods,* p. 352). Often it is poetically rendered: "You know something? It was beautiful. So still you could hear one aspen leaf caressing another, the moon wide and white shining through the leaves, and just above the dark, somber spruce, bunched closely together, tall and still like a crowd of black-robed monks standing in prayer" (*Ride the Dark Trail,* p. 164). Usually setting is integrated with action: "The way led up a draw between low, grassy hills. Before us the land grew rough, off to our right lay a vast sweep of plains, rolling gently away to an horizon lost in cloud. Huge thunderheads bulked high, a tortured dark blue mass that seemed to stir and move, but flat beneath where lightning leaped earthward" (*The Ferguson Rifle,* p. 98). L'Amour is a literary naturalist: many of his nature paintings imply the deterministic irony that beneath a golden but indifferent sky man purposefully conducts affairs that are puny at best: "It was such a pleasant day, the sun made leaf shadows on the ground around, and a few high, lazy clouds drifted in the sky. There was no violence around . . . except in that ring of silent guns, aimed at me" (*Mojave Crossing,* pp. 145–46). And from *Callaghen,* more tersely: "The mountains were on their right, raw, hard-edged mountains of rock thrust up from the desert floor, neither friendly or unfriendly, only indifferent" (p. 19).

When L'Amour describes Western nature, he often includes animals. The hero of *The Proving Trail* is traveling by railroad: "We rumbled over a bridge, slowed down for some reason, and I looked out to see the sun was down, the sky streaked with red, and a herd of antelope keeping pace with the train" (p. 133). L'Amour's favorite animal is the horse, about which we learn much in the course of reading his total production. Tell Sackett buys some Appaloosas, in *Treasure Mountain:* "There were three of them, sixteen hands, beautifully built, and in fine shape. One was a gray with a splash of white with black spots on the right shoulder, and a few spots freckled over the hips, black amidst the gray. The other horses were both black with splashes of white on the hips and the usual spots of the appaloosa" (pp. 55–56). L'Amour rightly opines that horses are at least as good as most human beings, are faithful if trusted, are "homebodies" even when allegedly wild, and upon being talked to can "sense . . . the kinship of interests if no more" (*The Lonesome Gods,* pp. 230, 236). More menacingly, "there are [we read] few things more terrible in battle than an infuriated mustang stallion" (*Down the Long Hills,* p. 53). L'Amour, in keeping with his desire to be the poor man's encyclopedist of the Far West, lectures us on the traits of other animals as well. We learn much about bears, cougars, dogs, mules, porcupines, wolverines, wolves, and the like, as well as bees, buzzards, eagles, jays, etc.

Characters

This teeming Western Eden L'Amour populates also with a variety of people. His typical hero is broad-shouldered, thin-hipped, military in bearing (and often in experience), taciturn but capable of poetic utterance, and possessed of a philosopher's appreciation of scene and beast—and woman. He is always a fighter, even a berserker if aroused—but often reluctant, rarely throwing the first punch or bullet. He fights with fists as often as with firearms, can take enormous punishment and retaliate with swift precision. A typical pattern of heroic reaction is biting, muted words; fisticuff flurry, ending in broken nose of antagonist; then deadly gunplay.

The first five heroes in L'Amour's long fiction establish the major characteristics, the best figures being Hondo Lane (*Hondo*) and Kilkenny (*Kilkenny*). Later heroes are better read, almost always—as with their creator—through a program of self-education. But their greatest virtues are neither prowess in fighting nor intellectual strength. They are, rather, the ability to adapt to nature's contours, physical, moral, and spiritual; willingness to learn from that great Western teacher, silence; and such commoner traits as patience, loyalty, and humor.[5]

L'Amour's heroines are best when they are aware that, although males and females may be equal in his world, the West was still a man's world, in which the best women walk beside not behind their men (as L'Amour images them with numbing monotony) while those men hold compass and map, and point the way. His heroines are regularly attractive, often with red, red-brown, or red-gold hair, and with gentle hands.[6] They are spunky, learn to fend for themselves and even defend themselves when necessary, are best—as is Shakespeare's Cordelia— when they speak softly (while carrying a long rifle); and they are maternal. In fact, L'Amour even while trying to keep up with the women's liberation movement says repeatedly that the function of women is to make babies and homes, while that of men is to nurture such homes in all good ways. Typical of dozens of such comments is one in *The Mountain Valley War* to the effect that "just as the maternal instinct is the strongest a woman has, just so the instinct to protect is the strongest in a man" (p. 10). Here is his anthropological follow-up: "It was man's natural instinct, bred from the ages before men were even men, to protect the family" (p. 87). As for women, we read in *The Quick and the Dead* that "[t]hey were practical. Their very nature as bearers of children made them so. For whenever they looked at a man there must always be the subconscious question of whether that man could take care of her and her children" (p. 75).

As for villains? They upset nature itself, because they grab and despoil land, in the process subverting the efforts of home-seeking heroes and home-making women. Further, villains are dishonorable in their modes of fighting. They hire underlings, whose vacillating loyalty is purchased not earned. They shoot from ambush. Worse, they tell lies. Now, when the hero lies, it is for a good cause and hence is justifiable. But when the villain lies, he does so to spread evil ("evil" being an old-fashioned word surprisingly common in L'Amour) and hence is hateful. Often the hero is naively upfront in his premature announcement of strategy, if not of tactics.

Structure

It should not be expected that L'Amour, given his haphazard style of composition, would craft novels having the architectural symmetry of, say, *The Scarlet Letter, The Portrait of a Lady, The Red Badge of Courage,* or *The Great Gatsby.* No, L'Amour is more like a hasty Impressionistic painter, leaving spots of canvas almost bare but loading on the color at points of emphasis; or he is perhaps like a romantic musical composer whose work has unbalanced parts but whose emotions are true, crashing.

L'Amour is best with his openings and with his endings. "Hit your reader on the chin. So he knows he's in a story. The reader doesn't want to know what's *going* to happen. He want[s] to know what's happening *now.* You've got to get the reader in the first two minutes," L'Amour advised a writing conference audience in 1967.[7] The statement assumes that a reader's attention span is short. It makes a mockery of the device of foreshadowing. It implies that the best way to sustain reader interest is by serial climaxing. And it implies that dénouements must be held to moments only.

Sometimes a L'Amour opening is an awakening. "A brutal kick in the ribs jolted him from a sound sleep and he lunged to his feet" (*The Iron Marshal,* p. 1). Sometimes we start with a mystery. "He lay sprawled upon the concrete pavement of the alley in the darkening stain of his own blood, a man I had never seen before. . ." (*The Broken Gun,* p. 1). Or with trouble. "It was Indian country, and when our wheel busted, none of them would stop" (*To Tame a Land,* p. 1). Or with a tragedy. "Smoke lifted from the charred timbers where once the house had stood. . ." (*The Mountain Valley War,* p. 1).

In some of his best openings L'Amour starts, breathlessly, in medias res. "My name is Tatton Chantry and unless the gods are kind to rogues, I shall die within minutes" (*Fair Blows the Wind,* p. 1); and "What I hoped for was a fat bear, and what I came up with was a skinny Indian" (*The Warrior's Path*. p. 1). As for the former novel, Tatton is not a rogue but an enemy of rogues, and being narrator he will survive as surely as will Herman Melville's Ishmael and Mark Twain's Huckleberry Finn. As for the latter novel, the comic tone is instantly belied and not repeated later. The opening of *Treasure Mountain* is cute and then puzzling, partly because we are given the names of six characters on the first page.[8]

One of L'Amour's most besetting midnovel problems is the use of foreshadowing, or rather his misuse of deceptive nonforeshadowing. Of fully a hundred examples, here is a simple one from *Borden Chantry*. Early in the novel the heroic lawman says of the unknown murderer, "I'm never going to quit until we get this man in jail" (p. 14). Some readers may feel entitled to guess that the killer will be jailed, may perhaps escape even, and then—? But it never happens. I conclude that L'Amour plants not only what become foreshadowing signposts on his fictive terrain—he does it often throughout *Lonely on the Mountain,* for example—but also deceptive path markers, simply because he does not know in advance just how his plots will turn out and, as he boasts, never rewrites. The less Shakespeare he!

I am not sure whether L'Amour's device of alternating first-person limited narrative point of view with omniscient point of view is brilliant or sloppy. It can result in heightened reader interest, in his occasional sense of superiority over the leading participants in the action, and in authorial irony—as in *Galloway,* for one example among a considerable number. But sometimes, as between chapters 8 and 9 of *The Sackett Brand,* the switch from limited to omniscient point of view is wrenchingly sudden. In more than one novel, the ventriloquial author forgets which voice he is using: three times in *Ride the River* L'Amour calls Echo Sackett, his narrator through much of the action, "she" (pp. 107, 114, 179) when "she" should be "I." Narrator Tell Sackett in *Lonely on the Mountain* is thrice called "he" (p. 188).

One of L'Amour's most skillful plot mechanisms is the vectoring of action lines. A representative example may be located in chapter 18 of *The High Graders,* in which the hero with a tough but untested little crew starts over a ridge with forty mules carrying gold, which the villain, followed by a secondary villain (who alerts the hero's turncoat friend), aims to intercept; meanwhile, a crony of the main villain, having kidnapped the heroine, rides by with her, paralleling the hero's route. Other examples are almost diagrammable in their cinematic neatness. Akin to vectoring is the plot pivot, a sudden dramatic swing in the direction of the action. For three neat examples: the hero of *Sitka* learns suddenly that he is going to Russia; Tell in *The Lonely Men* returns from his ordeal in Apacheria only to be arrested on a trumped-up but plausible murder charge; and this shocking request: "Kilkenny, I want you to kill my son!" (*The Rider of Lost Creek*, p. 123). Sometimes a pivot is hammered into the exact center of a novel, as when, for example, in the middle of chapter 7 of thirteen-chapter *Brionne* frightened little Mat turns happy just as his father Major James Brionne spies out the two separate bands of his pursuers.

As L'Amour rushes his action toward the climax, he often marshals events with comic-strip simplicity. Note for two examples the late-chapter events in *Killoe* (three deaths close to the hero in the penultimate chapter), and the jammed-up late action in *Reilly's Luck* (the hero is busy ruining the villain at poker while the villainess's gunman stalks the hero, also in the penultimate chapter). Such plotting results in crashing climaxes. Examples of such climaxes are too numerous to pick from easily. Here is a representatively revealing comment. Johannes Verne, narrator and hero of *The Lonesome Gods*, says toward the end of his epic struggle—against natural forces, evil men, ignorance and prejudice, and the demands of love—"It all was falling together at last" (p. 433).

L'Amour advises neophyte fiction writers to point every stylistic and plot ingredient toward the end, and then sign off with "a smile, a laugh, or a chuckle."[9] He follows his own advice well, as every L'Amour buff will swear—though whether creating a chuckle or an incredulous little gasp depends on that reader. Consider, as instances, the quite different closures of *Sitka*, *Kilrone*, *The Cherokee Trail*, *Matagorda*, and *The Man Called Noon*.

Words

What L'Amour uses to build his quick structures with are thousands upon thousands of words. Although his vocabulary is regularly a rather basic English, he does also illustrate precision of diction; in addition, his word hoard is enriched by foreign and technical words, Western localisms, certain significantly repeated key words, and crisp similes and metaphors.

A list of foreign Western words used by L'Amour (sometimes italicized, often not) would be very long. But a leading few might be: "agave," "alcalde," "arrastra," "bailes," "bisnaga," "brea," "calderas," "carreta," "cholla," "chosa," "chia," "cienaga," "cirque," "ephedra," "fandango," "galleta," "gruila," "hediondilla," "huisache," "jacal," "javelina," "manzanita," "maté," "ocotillo," "olla," "pakuru," "panocha," "pescadero," "pinole," "playa," "quesadilla," "ramuda," "rebozo," "rincon," "sahuaro," "saleratus," "segundo," "sipapu," "stupa," "thamnosma," "tinaja," "tornillo," "trincheras," "talus," "vaquero," "yucca,"[10] "zanja," and "zanza." Many Western buffs will recognize many of these words, but I would venture to say that no one can define them all.[11]

L'Amour loves aspects of Western scientific study, especially geological and horticultural. Therefore, many scientific terms come into play in his works. We appropriately find on one page (p. 131) of the mining novel *Comstock Lode* the following: quartz, calcite, galena, pyrite, argentite, and sphalerite. But it seems odd when wise-enough but semiliterate Tell Sackett, narrator of several Sackett novels, tosses around complex geological terms, as he occasionally does. For example, in *The Lonely Men* he discusses, between colloquial barrages, "faulted" earth, "quartz veins," "cretaceous bed[s]," "diorite," and "dikes that intruded" (p. 166).[12]

Key words in L'Amour, some repeated enough to make a psychologist wonder why they cluster so, include the following: "accept," "almighty" (as an intensive), "bait of food," "evil," "eyes,"[13] "fate," "field of fire," "good," "home," "hunch" (feeling, instinct, notion, sixth sense), "lie" (i.e., recline, often in a wrong grammatical form), "listen," "lonely," "loyal," "patience," "responsibility," "shoulders," "silence," "stand," "trouble,"[14] "water," and "will" (noun). Taken together and studied, these words help us picture an author (not simply his narrators) as colloquial, concerned with raw good and evil, not believing totally in fate but also in will power, observant and conscious of broad-built men, military, respectful of basics, aware of manifold dangers, and in awe of Western silence.

L'Amour admires heroism. The hero of *The Man Called Noon* ponders: "He felt no animosity toward anyone, nor any desire to do evil. Yet, did evil men ever think of themselves as evil?" (p. 37). Home is the implicit far-off goal of almost every major L'Amour hero, just as it was the explicit end toward which wily Ulysses wandered, especially when weary and wayworn. Like all good Westerners, L'Amour trusts his hunches, and so do his sensible characters—male, female, old, young, and juvenile.[15] Loneliness was endemic in the underpopulated West of the nineteenth century; hence it is a common word in

L'Amour. Loyalty, patience, and a sense of responsibility are cardinal
American virtues, often recently honored in the breach; but they are,
perhaps for that reason, as common an element in the typical L'Amour
hero and heroine as blood and bone. Being big and broad-shouldered
himself, L'Amour regularly delineates his big heroes after happily looking into a full-length mirror. Tell Sackett, for example, ranges from 6'
2" to even taller, only a bit over the height at which his interviewers
peg L'Amour himself.

Poetic Prose

Having first published as a poet (though a very bad one), L'Amour
naturally enough employs many similes and a fair number of metaphors
in his prose, which is also sometimes poetically rhythmic. Like a good
Westerner, he uses images from poker more than from any other category. Most such tropes are routine, but the following is special: covered
from doorway and window by rifles, Tucker comes up with a pair of
puns, and says, "I never draw against a full house" (*Tucker*, p. 68).
Since Western action often seems symbolized by poker—with uncoop-
erative players, a combination of luck and skill and bluff, and marked
by habitual taciturnity—rather than by pro-Eastern chess, it is not
surprising that L'Amour employs few chess figures, and none exciting.
Thus: "circumstances were moving men on the chessboard" (*The Empty
Land*, p. 25), and "He had liked playing his chess game with the law"
(*Son of a Wanted Man*, p. 59).

The four most common images in L'Amour describe rain as like a
mesh of metal, creek water as chuckling, stars as lamps, and stealthy
movement as ghostlike. So we have these: "The driving rain drew a
sullen, metallic curtain across the fading afternoon" (*Radigan*, p. 1);
"The stream chuckled along over the stones" (*Treasure Mountain*, p. 93);
"I could . . . see the morning star hanging in the sky like a light in a
distant window" (*The Lonesome Gods*, p. 52); and "Instantly he clapped
the spurs to his mount and went ghosting through the trees" (*The
Mountain Valley War*, p. 166). The crispest image in all of L'Amour, to
my mind, is this refreshing notion, occasionally repeated: "The air was
fresh and cool, so much so it was like drinking water from a spring
just to breathe it" (*Bendigo Shafter*, p. 89). Less effective is the way half
the hungry men in L'Amour say "My stomach thinks my throat's been
cut" (*The Shadow Riders*, p. 37, etc.). Hardly better is calling a would-

be hard man not even "a pimple on a tough man's neck" (*Bendigo Shafter,* p. 165), as L'Amour does too often.

Sunset and trees evoke some of L'Amour's finest figurative effects. For but three examples among scores: "The sky was shot with flaming arrows that slowly faded, leaving a kiss of crimson on the edges of clouds, and the prairie itself turned a sullen red, darkening into shadows and the night" (*The Ferguson Rifle,* p. 21); "the great swell of the mountain . . . [had] a battalion of aspens marching down the slope in a solid rank til [*sic*] it came to a halt . . . [l]ike a troupe [*sic*] of soldiers"; and "The sentinel pines stood straight and dark, austere as nuns at prayer" (*Over on the Dry Side,* pp. 16, 158).

Here are a half dozen assorted little splendors: "Slowly my thoughts sifted the names and faces through the sieve of recollection" (*The Man from the Broken Hills,* p. 130). "If you're going to have steam in the kettle [male sexual arousal], you've got to have fire in the stove [female attractiveness]" (*Rivers West,* p. 81). "He was . . . friendly but reserved, standing a cool sentry before the doors of his personal life" (*Borden Chantry,* p. 107). "Trevallion turned the thought on the spit on his mind" (*Comstock Lode,* p. 392). "Yet slowly caution began to slip through the cracks in his ego" (*Ride the River,* p. 20). And finally this one, which describes all of L'Amour's heroes, half of his heroines, and himself: "I thought of them then, those four young men who rode with me, four young men carved from the . . . oak of trouble" (*The Lonesome Gods,* p. 341).

Akin to imagery in L'Amour is his occasional, very effective use of an almost scannably rhythmic prose. This pleasant practice may crop out anywhere; but it is especially noticeable in *The Ferguson Rifle, To the Far Blue Mountains, Fair Blows the Wind,* and *The Warrior's Path.* Thus, we have "No other rides with me, and the plains lie vast about" (*The Ferguson Rifle,* p. 1); and "Green lay the coast and gray the sea" (*To the Far Blue Mountains,* p. 92). Such basic rhythms enhanced by alliteration are doubly appealing, as in "Dust devils danced upon the desert's face" (*The Mountain Valley War,* p. 124), or "deep were the depths into which it descended" (*The High Graders,* p. 25).

Humor

Most Western writers are humorists. L'Amour is almost an exception. His grasp on Western history is perhaps too serious. When he makes up for lost time and tries to strike a comic tone, as in *Fallon*, he can be momentarily effective. And the cocky young narrator of "What Gold Does to a Man," reprinted in *Buckskin Run*, quickly establishes a comic voice and sustains it fairly well to the end. But usually such efforts are short-lived. At the same time, L'Amour's seriously challenged characters make highly humorous asides. One might almost say that his characters, and even some of his first-person narrators, can be funny while L'Amour is mainly not.

Matagorda, chapter 6, has a pleasant sequence of comic range-talk by cowboys around a herd. *Chancy, Conagher, Where the Long Grass Blows,* and *Milo Talon*, among a few other titles, feature a good deal of humorous lingo. Much verbal fun derives from guns and danger. Here are common examples: "I'll put a bullet where your breakfast is"; "But I am *not* alone; I have my rifle"; "We are too short to be worth shooting and tanning"; "They could not shoot him, because they aimed at his heart and he didn't have any"; "Your body would be a soft bunk for my bullets"; "My jury has twelve bullets"; and the like. Since the purpose of funny gunmen is to commit homicide, death, too, can be the subject of jokes on the range: "He had no idea he was dead"; "He was as dead as any man can get"; "He is such a big corpse he will spoil fast"; "I'll put another hole in your face to feed you through"; "Let's shoot him a little and then hang him"; etc.

L'Amour is an almost immaculately "clean" writer; still, we do find some comic language having to do with sex: "But you've got to admit she keeps what she's got so you know it's there" (*Mojave Crossing*, pp. 102–3); "[T]hat girl left her horse a-flyin' and busted a pretty little dent in the ground when she hit stern first" (*The Sky-Liners*, p. 14); "The man into whose lap I'd kicked the [boiling] coffeepot had troubles enough. He was jumping around like mad and I could see I'd ruined his social life for some time to come" (*Ride the Dark Trail*, p. 33); "[T]emper passion with wisdom, my son, for sometimes the glands speak louder than the brain" (*Sackett's Land*, p. 18). Not much, I admit.

Sometimes L'Amour's humor sounds traditionally Southwestern, with typical Twainesque exaggeration and deadpan. Here are three examples: "He was so thin he would have to stand twice in the same place to make a shadow" (*Chancy*, p. 52); "There were men came into that place so rough they wore their clothes out from the inside first" (*The Lonely Men*, p. 28); and "He was a gnarled and wizened old man with a face that looked old enough to have worn out two bodies" (*The Man Called Noon,* p. 149).

The funniest sequence, in my view, in all of L'Amour comes when a bunch of cowpokes are discussing Shakespeare: "Gatty took a gulp of coffee. 'That Shakespeare, now, I think he *borrowed* a lot here and there. Why, ever' once in a while I'd come on things in his plays that I'd heard folks sayin' for years. All he did was write them down'" (*Hanging Woman Creek,* p. 71).

So Shakespeare is full of clichés? Well, so is L'Amour. Sometimes he takes them and adapts them for humorous purposes, as with "he would fight at the drop of a hat, and drop it himself" (often used); or "He was dead-and-buried tired" (*The Man from Skibbereen,* p. 161); "It was not a shotgun wedding, rather, a shotgun departure"; "He was getting hot under the collar but had no collar"; and this good advice, Don't "beat . . . around the greasewood" (*Silver Canyon,* p. 6). Unfortunately, L'Amour often uses verbal chestnuts without poetic elaboration that would achieve freshness. Some of these phrases are merely Western conversational neutralities, such as "I'm forever damned," "since who flung the chunk," "shot with luck," "shot to doll rags," "light a shuck," "rattle your hocks," "you know the drill," "by the Lord Harry," "hell on wheels with a gun" ("hell on a bicycle" once), "the brassy sky," "that coffee would float a horseshoe," "open the ball," "bite the bullet," "curly wolf," "that really shines," "don't waste around," "in a tight," "light an' set," "I should smile," "a long-geared man," "he would charge hell with a bucket of water," "hold the fort," "on the prod," "loaded for bear," "I saddle my own broncs," and "he's a man to ride the river with."

Just as often, L'Amour too hastily settles for a cliché—including a few he himself as created by dint of overuse—instead of striving for something new. All of which is a function of the speed with which this Western phenomenon composes and publishes. Thus we frequently encounter "one's tail in a crack," "that doesn't cut any ice," "there are tides in the affairs of men," "up the creek without a paddle," "not on your tintype," "root hog or die," "the riot act," "little pitchers have big ears," "not my cup of tea," "like shooting ducks in a barrel," "cut the mustard," "rub him out," "push up daisies," "a fate worse than death," "up a tree," "honey draws flies," "the fat is in the fire," "the chips are down," "naked as a jaybird," "fly the coop," "things that go bump in the night," "a wild-goose chase," "as Irish as Paddy's pig,"

"easy sailing," "a bee in her bonnet," "don't fly off the handle," and
"I'll tear down your meathouse." (Admittedly, a vast majority of these
hackneyed lines appear in dialogue in L'Amour.)

Taken en masse, these clichés might permit the conclusion that L'A-
mour is hasty and slipshod. Maybe he is. But the truth surely is that
he knows his audience. And his average reader is undoubtedly pleased
by the sense of verbal familiarity that clichés help to generate as he
reads merrily along, happy as a lark, on pins and needles while suspense mounts until the villain gets his comeuppance.[16]

Little Errors

It may be forgivable, in the name of high sales figures, for L'Amour
to employ a hundred quick clichés instead of slowly striving for effects
more memorable. But his compositional errors, though rarely serious,
are another matter. The man boasts of being self-educated. Further, he
advises his readers that a program of private study can educate them as
thoroughly as fireside perusal of Plutarch and Blackstone tutored some
of his imaginary bronc-busters. But the truth is that L'Amour commits
just about every common error pointed out in basic writing courses. I
hate to say this about a Western novelist whose works I have been
engrossed by and admire; but L'Amour, rather like Stephen Crane and
the early Faulkner, could have profited from basic freshman English
instruction. It may be true, as L'Amour repeatedly informs us in his
fiction, that "Many . . . teachers know nothing" (*The Proving Trail*, p.
108); but most English teachers, unlike L'Amour, avoid committing
the following errors in composition. (Given space limitations, I cite
only one or two examples under each category, from dozens and scores
of possible choices. And admittedly, some of these errors appear in
folksy dialogue, but L'Amour commits all of the following errors in
his own right as well.)

Antecedent disagreement: "each person is alone within their minds"
(*Matagorda*, p. 119). "Centered" misused: "Genester's hopes center
around [i.e., on] the old man" (*Sackett's Land*, p. 53). "Cannot help
but": "I could not help but remember" (*The Warrior's Path*, p. 144).
Dangling modifiers: "Crawling in, there was room enough. . . .
Walking on, night came" (*The Lonesome Gods*, p. 91); "Byrd's book was
written while surveying" (*Frontier*, p. 99).[17] "Due to" misused: "due to
long drives . . . they'd lost weight" (*Lonely on the Mountain*, p. 131).
"Equally as": "he was to choose an alternative hide-out equally as well

hidden" (*How the West Was Won*, p. 235). "Further" for "farther": "He would find the right place somewhere farther on, and from that point he would go no further" (*Brionne*, p. 104).

"Kind of a" and "sort of a": "I'd no idea what kind of a fix I was in. . . . [H]e did not know . . . what kind of a mood I was in" (*Milo Talon*, p. 170); "her mind was working swiftly toward some sort of a solution" (*The Iron Marshal*, p. 166). "Lay" for "lie," etc.: "he avoided a hard look at whatever future might lay ahead of him" (*The High Graders*, p. 42), etc. "Not un-": "The story was not unfamiliar" (*Dark Canyon*, p. 11).[18] Number errors: "the story of your pursuit of Zachary Verne and your daughter are well know" (*The Lonesome Gods*, p. 423); "one of the things that has protected me" (*The Rider of Lost Creek*, p. 121). "Only" misplaced: "I've only read [not understood?] Plutarch [and no other author?] four [not five?] times" (*To Tame a Land*, p. 152). "Outside of": "By eight-thirty you should be outside of town" (*The Proving Trail*, p. 145). Parallelism violated: "but I wanted neither to be shot at by those I wished to help, nor by those searching for them" (*The Ferguson Rifle*, p. 75).

Pronoun misuse: "yet the urge was on us, and on Abby no less than I"; and "Building with logs was a foreign thing to we of England" (*To the Far Blue Mountains*, pp. 194, 218). "[T]hey had to do with he who screamed?" (*Milo Talon*, p. 65). "[A]s for she herself" (*Shalako*, p. 50). "And do not be like an oyster who rests on the sea bottom" (*The Lonesome Gods*, p. 32). "[I]t was Devoy, whom he had heard was a good man" (*Borden Chantry*, p. 163). "Reason is because": "The only reason I interfered was because the man was so obviously a crook" (*Fallon*, p. 100). Split infinitives: "The first [problem] was to obtain the wherewithal to even live, to exist" (*Fair Blows the Wind*, p. 136). Squinting modifiers: "I could hobble only using the crutch" (*The Walking Drum*, p. 308). "That" doubled: "she had no doubt that after he had stayed with her as much as he wanted that he would kill her" (*Radigan*, p. 143). "There" misused: "There were better grazing lands available" (*Dark Canyon*, p. 16); "there's hard feelings among their riders" (*Where the Long Grass Blows*, p. 97). "Try and": "there was nothing to be done except to try and spot any man carrying a package" (*Kilrone*, p. 108). Finally the minor but common syntactical error that I call "x and that y," as in "They said I had no choice. Some men had been murdered and that I would also be killed" (*Milo Talon*, p. 128).

Related to composition errors are L'Amour's substantive mistakes, such as renaming a given character or place, miscounting animals or wounds or corpses, getting the year wrong, and the like. Typos are another source of annoyance to the harmless pedagogical reader: "cool-ly" is mispelled as "cooly" nine times in *Where The Long Grass Blows,* for one example. There are more than a dozen typos and punctuation oddities in *Bendigo Shafter;* more than a score in *Fair Blows the Wind.*

Books

L'Amour continually informs his readers that his ill-schooled heroes and heroines can gain instant wisdom by reading in their spare time. Thus, in *The Daybreakers* Orrin Sackett is taught to read and write by Tom Sunday, is inspired by stories of Davy Crockett and Andrew Jackson (who though illiterate into manood made it in politics), impresses Tom later by casually remarking that he likes Charles Dickens, and still later is remembered thus by his admiring brother Tell: "Orrin had started early to reading law, packing a copy of Blackstone in his saddlebags and reading whenever there was time" (*Treasure Mountain,* pp. 9–10).

In *To Tame a Land* a well-read older man gives his surrogate son, the narrator-hero, a book, saying, "Read it. . . . Read it five times. You'll like it better each time. It's some stories about great men, and more great men have read this book than any other" (p. 18). The book? Plutarch, which by chapter 4 the narrator says he is reading for the fourth time. By chapter 10, "Only four, so far. But I'll get to it" (p. 84). Eight chapters later he distracts the book-giver, by now his mortal enemy, with the confession that he has still read the book only four times, then kills him.[19]

L'Amour's novel citing the most books is surely *Bendigo Shafter,* in which Ruth Mackin wagons a choice library of fifty volumes west of the Dakotas. It includes Josiah Gregg, Meriwether Lewis and William Clark, Washington Irving, Nelson Lee, Henry David Thoreau,[20] Plutarch, John Locke, Michel Eyquem de Montaigne, William Bartram, Alexis de Tocqueville, John Stuart Mill, David Hume, William Blackstone, and Timothy Dwight. Also mentioned as making up Bendigo's reading fare are Charles Barras, Dion Boucicault, Edward Bulwer-Lytton, Bret Harte, Juvenal, Anna Cora Mowatt, Nathaniel Hawthorne, Edgar Allan Poe, and William Shakespeare.[21]

Another bookish book is *Reilly's Luck.* Its hero Val reads Alfred, Lord Tennyson, Sir Walter Scott, Johannes Wolfgang von Goethe, Lord Byron, the Comte de Volney, John Gibson Lockhart, Charles Kingsley,

Plato, David Hume, John Locke, George Berkeley, Baruch Spinoza, Voltaire, and Robert Burton. Burton's *Anatomy of Melancholy* literally saves Val's life: when a villain fires twice at the hero he is turning from a bookshelf with Burton's thick tome in his hand, and it stops the bullets. Val jokes: "I was never able to get through this book myself" (p. 159).[22]

How many of these classics has L'Amour been able to get through himself? He must be, by all odds, the most seemingly bookish of all popular Western writers. But the fact remains that the writers who have influenced him the most are not the titans of literature, many of whom he mentions merely in passing, as we have seen. Instead, they are short-story craftsmen. L'Amour once recalled that after getting a few hundred rejection slips for stories about boxing, football, rodeos, and history, he suddenly wondered why: "when none of them [the stories] were selling, I decided all the editors wouldn't be crazy; something had to be wrong with what I was doing. So I got a half-dozen stories by O. Henry, [Guy] de Maupassant, Robert Louis Stevenson and others I liked . . . and I went over them very carefully, step-by-step, to see what they were doing that I wasn't doing. Shortly after that I began to sell."[23]

Western History

Louis L'Amour is an exceedingly didactic author. He offers his readers facts—often trivial—and direct opinions on a surprising variety of subjects. He habitually pauses in his story-telling to present informative asides, to tender advice, and to generalize. In doing so, he discusses history, frontier survival, pragmatic philosophy, love, and family life.[24]

L'Amour takes seriously his role as a self-appointed Western encyclopedist. A list of subjects on which he gives information would include: animals, anthropology, clothes, the East (urban, overregulated, comparatively effete), echoes (animal, bird, human), fighting (boxing, dueling, shooting), geology, gypsies, hotels, hunting, Indians, judging distances, Madeira wine, the Middle East and the Far East, moccasins, nail-making, patrons in Elizabethan England, sailing, saloons, slavery (world-wide), soldiers and soldiering, the Swiss militia, tin horns, transportation, underwater salvage, weapons (bows and arrows, clubs, knives, stones, swords, revolvers, rifles), the weather, and above all Western life.

The subject L'Amour likes to tell his readers about the most, both directly and indirectly, is Western American history.[25] Most of his stories may be placed and dated to a degree. Often a particular scene has a real mountain, river, trail, fort, or town in it and is hence locatable on the map.[26] Often the action rushes forward against a historical backdrop typically sketched in with just a few brush strokes. Always, L'Amour concentrates on his fictional characters and their activities. But his process—his success formula, if you will—permits the inclusion of geographical and historical background reality. One of his most effective "lessons" comes during a pause in the action of *Over on the Dry Side,* during which scholarly Owen Chantry lectures an ironically reluctant listener, the callow narrator, about Ute Indians in the region, and Navajos nearby, the latter's migratory habits eight centuries before, Indian ghost houses by the shelf of the Mesa Verde, with the Sleeping Ute Mountains against the distant horizon.[27]

Another nice touch in L'Amour is his identifying early explorers of various regions. In his beloved Southwest they are naturally enough Spaniards, as fans of the Sackett series can attest. Tell Sackett gives his sensitive readers a thrill when he mentions Father Silvestre Escalante and Fernando Rivera, and casually reports finding a Spanish grave in Ute country: "Maybe [he adds] I was the first to see that grave in three hundred years" (*Sackett,* p. 17). Other long-gone explorers include northern European travelers, mostly British. L'Amour honors seemingly illiterate local characters by making them repositories of historical lore, as when one oldtimer warns a tenderfoot heading farther west: "Don't envy you, young feller. . . . You got a long road to travel. . . . Oh, there's folks done it! [John] Palliser done it, the Earl of Southesk, he done it, and, of course, folks like David Thompson, Alexander Henry, and the like. . . " (*Lonely on the Mountain,* p. 55). I'd say the old coot had been foraging in L'Amour's L.A. library.

Fort after fort, small towns, buildings therein, and western cities once rowdy and gaudy—for example, Denver—but now tame, all come under L'Amour's careful scrutiny and emerge vivified on his pages. What distinguishes L'Amour from most other writers of Western fiction may well be the historical verisimilitude with which he presents his locales, both natural and manmade. Another may be the somewhat awkward manner he has of handling references to Western outlaws. For a particularly ineffective example, consider the thoughts running through the mind of the gunman hero of *The Mountain Valley War,* about to enter a town to clean it up pronto. "Riding in was going to be much easier than getting out. None knew him here, to be awed by his reputation. Anyway, the old days were passing. One heard little of Ben Thompson or King Fisher. Billy the Kid had been killed by Pat Garrett, Virgil Earp had killed Billy Brooks. Names of men once mighty in the west were sliding into the grave or into oblivion" (p. 21). So?

L'Amour is at his best in using real-life characters when he does so only casually, for example when Wyatt Earp and Bat Masterson make cameo appearances in *The Sky-Liners* (already noted). When he tries to fictionalize an important Western historical character in detail, he fails—as with Cullen Baker, hero of *The First Fast Draw* (already discussed).[28]

Indians

To my mind, the most vital and controversial Western subjects in all of L'Amour are Indians, women, and the West as a microcosm of conservative America.

An entire monograph could be written on L'Amour and the Indian. Its three-pronged thesis would surely be that Indians are good and bad, just like all other branches of the human family; that their way of life has given Indians a set of values often at variance with those of white men and women; and that since the beginning of human history, migration of peoples has occurred, and that, therefore, the Indians of the American West could call the land theirs only so long as they could successfully defend it. L'Amour has maintained these tenets through at least half a hundred fictional works, and his reasoning is tough and logical; but he derives much of it from nineteenth-century sources, not twentieth-century ones. He is therefore to be regarded as ultraconservative, anathema to modern revisionists, but probably for those reasons all the more popular with his mass readership.[29]

Typifying L'Amour's attitude is this address of a veteran to a tenderfoot: "Ma'am, . . . Injuns are folks. They're like you an' me. . . . Some you can trust; some you can't. There's just as many honest folks among Injuns as among white or black. An' there's just as many thieves and liars" (*The Cherokee Trail,* p. 34).

L'Amour often pauses to lecture thus on Indians or to have a knowledgeable character do so. The two longest and best such mini-essays appear in *High Lonesome* and *Bendigo Shafter.* In *High Lonesome* (pp. 83–84) a canny old frontiersman explains that from the start the Indian was a warrior, with a cultural background at odds with that of the whites, with nonwhite behavioral standards, without mercy, enjoying horse-stealing, hunting, and mortal combat, amused by torture, impressed by courage (and also fortitude, strength, and cunning), puzzled by the weapons and persistence of whites, indifferent to seizing territory for the purpose of holding it. In *Bendigo Shafter* (pp. 261–62) the hero meets Horace Greeley in New York and, when queried about "the Indian situation," explains with the benefit of L'Amouresque hindsight that nothing can be done to avoid trouble with the Indians, whom he says most Western whites compare to the buffalo ("an obstacle to settlement of the land"); he then lectures on Indian hunting, war, horse-stealing, failure at trade, contempt for manual labor, and on the radical differences in Indian and white religions, customs, lifestyles, and value systems.

Employing his usual technique, L'Amour scatters little comments on Indians throughout much of his fiction. They are informative and vivid. We learn, for example, that time means little to Indians, they walk straight-footed, avoid fighting to the last man, "torture, not only to bring suffering to an enemy, but to test how much he could stand" (*Kid Rodelo,* pp. 62–63), take high trails typically, have superstitions based to a degree on good sense, like to talk, can spot one's weakness fast, have "angry blood" (*The Sky-Liners,* p. 91), treat children well, try to leave "no scars on the landscape" (*Conagher,* p. 42), avoid killing camp visitors, strive for prestige and resent contempt, sometimes have incredible eyesight, in rare cases practice cannibalism (*The Shadow Riders,* p. 129), have a sense of humor, and do not scare easily or for long. L'Amour often discusses prehistoric Indians, sometimes in exciting ways, comparing them as trail-makers to "the merchant caravans of the Middle Ages" (*Tucker,* p. 24). He suggests, as did Francis Parkman and other commentators even earlier, that "[t]he death of the red man's way came when the first white trader came among them to trade what the Indian could not himself make. . . . The needle, the steel knife blade, the gun and gunpowder, the whiskey, and the various ornaments. These were the seeds of his destruction, and what he warred against was the desire in his own heart. There were those who protested against using the white man's things, but their voices spoke into the hollow air, and no ear listened" (*Bendigo Shafter,* p. 95). L'Amour also voices the oft-repeated line that the High Plains Indians sent into the field the finest light cavalry the world has ever seen.

Women

L'Amour's running commentary on women in the West is dramatic, provocative, and inconsistent.[30] The topic might well be the subject of a long and valuable essay.[31] If L'Amour's leading comments were published as a brief handbook on ideal women and how they should handle men, it would conservatively counter a spate of recent books on how women can get more mileage out of their men.

It could begin: "Give me always a woman with pride, and pride of being a woman" (*The Warrior's Path,* p. 164); "Who knows what iron is in the heart of a woman?" (*The Lonesome Gods,* p. 432); "A man, he's got to get along mostly with hard work an' persistence, but with a woman it is mostly maneuver" (*Ride the River,* p. 94). L'Amour seems to equate feminine beauty with sex appeal; note the implications of the following comment: "despite her obvious beauty there was . . . a certain elusive charm that prevented the lips from being sensual" (*The Rider of Lost Creek,* p. 71). Every woman needs a man, L'Amour tells us with tedious repetition. So much the better if that man is lighthearted, for "A girl can always make do with a man who smiles from the heart" (*The Cherokee Trail,* p. 83). Women can smile from the heart too; we read that "No woman objects to a man looking the fool once in a while—makes 'em more human, somehow" (*How the West Was Won,* p. 83). Still, "It's a bad thing for a man to be shamed in front of his womenfolks. . . . It's sometimes worse than bein' killed" (*Catlow,* p. 46). The sexes really battle, don't they? "Gals like the high-spirited, high-headed kind [of men], I've noticed. If they can break them to harness they aren't at all what the gal wanted in the beginning, and if she can't break them they usually break her. But that's the way of it" (*Galloway,* p. 54). Twice L'Amour suggests that obstreperous women must be handled like fractious horses.[32]

As noted, L'Amour often says that woman instinctively want home and children, and that men want to build, hunt, provide, and otherwise protect the family unit. How to manage? "You know's well as I do if a woman sets her cap for a man he ain't got a chance. Only if he runs. That's all!" (*The Tall Stranger,* p. 92). It helps if the woman lacks passion: "He had seen her kind before—the ones who handled men the best because they lacked passion themselves. They were always thinking while a man was merely feeling" (*Flint,* p. 98).[33] Once she has snared her man, however, she should follow him: "If a woman loved a man she would live [with him] anywhere, anywhere at all" (*Taggart*, p. 148). Also, "if you [a certain young woman in love] marry him and want to be happy, you will have to grow with him" (*The Mountain Valley War*, p. 170). Behave so as to deserve to walk beside him, not behind him. L'Amour uses this marriage-as-stroll image dozens of times. Don't forget, though, you women. Here is a proper woman: "She did not ask questions, but did what he suggested [i.e., ordered]" (*The Man Called Noon*, p. 131). [34]

The rest of L'Amour's pronouncements concerning women, especially in the West, may be disposed of briefly. The author contradictorily says both that women could travel safely in the West, because of the high regard in which Western men held them, and also that women had to be protected, not merely from natural dangers but from bad men, who if they turned to molestation were quickly hanged—at least. He says not only that women are easily scared—and when so should not be trusted to make decisions—but also that they often can be trusted to handle adverse news with courage and dignity. He has one character say of women that "They're mostly in trouble, an' when they ain't, they're gettin' other folks into it" (*The Ferguson Rifle*, p. 134). Further, they enjoy gossiping about an event more than experiencing the event itself. Nevertheless, they have gentle hands, are useful at sick beds, and can certainly ease the inevitable when a hurt man is dying.

To close on a finer note, I report that when the polite hero of *The Iron Marshal* starts to interview a certain "pleasant-looking, attractive woman," we read this: "Had someone asked her what she was, she would have said, 'housewife,' and been proud of it" (p. 107). [35] Better is this ideal woman, the best in all of L'Amour's fiction: Ruth Mackin of *Bendigo Shafter* "had set a standard of womanhood against which every woman I later was to know [says narrator Shafter] would be unconsciously measured. She was quietly beautiful, moving with an easy grace and confidence. She was tolerant, understanding, and intelligent, a good listener ready with apt comment; she understood. . . . She had style. . ." (p. 300). [36]

General Advice

L'Amour is eternally stopping his narrative action to offer information on a thousand topics, advice on basic rugged human behavior, and glacial generalizations on life itself.

As we have partly seen, L'Amour is knowledgeable about minor corners of Western American history. In addition, he can be counted on to tell us about nature, animals, outdoor living, and the tools and weapons necessary for survival there. But he also lectures, sometimes gratuitously but often excitingly, on building undetectable campfires, boxing and wrestling, how to stab an opponent fatally, shooting, tracking, outguessing the criminal mind, the best methods of guerrilla and allied warfare, the treatment of wounds, the dangers of wealth, hatred, fear and bravery, parenting, education, ideals, loneliness, inevitable aging, mutability, and time. He also intermittently says beware, ye softening Americans of our crisis-riddled epoch.

If I were to choose twenty or so favorite L'Amouresque generalizations, the list would inevitably be askew. There are several hundred scattered through his works. Often they are spoken by fictional characters, who, however, seem usually to speak for L'Amour himself. What about the following? "We do not own the land. . . . We hold it in trust for tomorrow" (*Hondo,* p. 59). "The object . . . of any war is to destroy your enemy's fighting force" (*Utah Blaine,* p. 60). "Those loyalties were his life, his religion, his reason for living" (*Crossfire Trail,* p. 109). "Fear is not a bad thing. It is fear that saves men's lives . . . it prepares a man for trouble" (*Taggart,* p. 48). "[T]here was an end to everything" (*High Lonesome,* p. 126). "When evil takes up to violence, the good have no choice but to defend themselves" (*Hanging Woman Creek,* p. 94). "Liquor never solved any problem, nor did it make a problem more simple" (*Kiowa Trail,* p. 18). "One of the easiest ways to be brave is to have bravery expected of you." "Many troubles removed themselves if one merely waited" (*Kilrone,* pp. 59, 135). But also "The way to face trouble . . . was to meet it head-on" (*Brionne,* p. 95). "Man has within himself the most powerful weapon ever developed—the human brain." "[A]all [criminals] were incurable optimists, as well as egotists. They were confident their plans would succeed, and had nothing but contempt for the law and for the law-abiding citizen" (*The Broken Gun,* pp. 66, 95). "[T]here was no stoppin' a man who was set on an idea" (*Tucker,* p. 57). "[G]old is easier found than kept" (*Treasure Mountain,* p. 114). "And there is perhaps no one hated more by a man than one to whom he has done an injustice" (*Callaghen,* p. 38). "[W]ho was altogether honest?" (*The Man from Skibbereen,* p. 101). "Maybe a man shouldn't have it [wealth] when he's young. It robs him of something, gives him all he can have when he's too young to know what he's got" (*The Man from the Broken Hills,* p.

187). "[C]oincidence interferes in all our lives. . ." (*Rivers West*, p. 56).
"[N]o two men age at the same rate." "[I]n wisdom there is often pain"
(*To the Far Blue Mountains*, pp. 167, 214). "[G]rowth is ever accompanied by pain." "Regret is a vain thing" (*Fair Blows the Wind*, pp.
28, 200); "Many look but do not see." "[C]ivilization is a flimsy cloak"
(*Bendigo Shafter*, pp. 140, 244). "It is . . . as sinful not to believe in
the devil as not to believe in God! "[A]ll men can fail, and each man
must somewhere find his master, with whatever strength, whatever
weapon. So we must be wary. . . ." "There are slaves everywhere.
Many are slaves, one way or another, who do not realize they are. . . ."
"[T]here must be law . . . man must have order, and evil must be
restrained or punished" (*The Warrior's Path*, pp. 28, 36, 64, 90–91).
"All too often the man a girl thinks she loves or the girl a man believes
he loves is just in their imaginations." "Nothing was ever gained by
lying but the risk of more lies" (*Milo Talon*, pp. 139, 159). "The
strongest . . . is he who stands alone" (*The Cherokee Trail*, p. 75). "Did
not a man's enemies make a sharper, more decisive man of him?" (*The
Walking Drum*, p. 64).

Finally, I have a feeling that L'Amour, who is an intensely self-
conscious, self-aggrandizing phenomenon on our current literary scene,
generalizes often with the intention of projecting one image of himself
but sometimes with the result that he projects another image without
intending to do so. What is more valuable in the following generalizations than the picture we get from them of their author himself?

"Wealth is important only to the small of mind" (*Hondo*, p. 78),
and "it mattered little how much money a man had as long as he was
contented" (*The First Fast Draw*, p. 11). "He was, as are many self-
made men, curiously self-centered" (*Silver Canyon*, p. 53); and "He
carried himself with that impatient arrogance toward others that is
often possessed by men who have succeeded by their own efforts, and
too easily" (*The Sackett Brand*, p. 135). "Success corrodes" (*Galloway*,
p. 117); "Sometimes I think the further a man gets from the simple
basic needs the less happy he is" (*Under the Sweetwater Rim*, p. 92).
"[T]he ones who wind up on top are usually those with the most effi-
cient life style" (*Tucker*, p. 24). "Writing is a lonely business. . ." (*Fair
Blows the Wind*, p. 154).

And at last these tried old truisms: "[I]t is easier to dream than to
realize the dream" (*The Ferguson Rifle*, p. 15). "The trail is the thing,
not the end of the trail" (*Ride the Dark Trail*, p. 44). "Wherever a man
is, there is work to do. That's the best part of it" (*Bendigo Shafter*, p.

281). Ultimately does not all of L'Amour's fiction point to the conclusion imbedded in the following charming dialogue? It occurs just moments before the marriage ceremony of Barnabas Sackett and Abigail Tempany. Barnabas starts the talk.

"There is something about solemn occasions that always stirs my humor. I like them, I respect them, but sometimes I think we all take ourselves too seriously."

"You don't think marriage is serious?"

"Of course, I do. It is the ultimate test of maturity. . . ." (*To the Far Blue Mountains,* p. 138)

The good-humored maturity of Louis Dearborn L'Amour has evolved out of a humble adolescence, a rollicking early youth marked by jobs in various fields and aboard many ships, global war, and decades of intense writing—writing that is surely best when it is about the American West. He knows its past, its people, and its geography. He is happiest at work, meeting countless readers of his melodramatic fiction, with friends in California and Colorado, and above all with his family at home.

Notes and References

(Citations of works obvious in context are made parenthetically in the text.)

Chapter One

1. Jon Tuska and Vicki Piekarski, eds., *Encyclopedia of Frontier and Western Fiction* (New York: McGraw-Hill, 1983), *passim*.

2. Candace Klaschus, "Louis L'Amour: The Writer as Teacher," Ph.D. diss., University of New Mexico, 1983, 34.

3. Barbara A. Bannon, "Louis L'Amour," *Publishers Weekly* 204 (8 October 1973):56. L'Amour regards himself as the common man's encyclopedia of the West and also as an expert on six thousand years of history—Hank Nuwer, "Louis L'Amour: Range Writer," *Country Gentleman* 130 (Spring 1979):99; Suzy Kalter, "Louis L'Amour: He Tells How the West Was Really Won," *Family Weekly*, 10 June 1979, 7. The Talon family was originally to be named Sigourney; "Research, World-Wide Experience Grist for Mill of Frontier Author," *North Dakota Motorist*, March-April 1972, 4.

4. For LaMoore family information I rely mainly on four sources: 1) Edna LaMoore Waldo, L'Amour's older sister, whose unpaged, handwritten manuscripts (now at the Alfred Dickey Library, Jamestown, North Dakota)—"LaMoore Family Background: 1862–1863, 1882"; "Edna LaMoore Waldo: Jamestown, 1893: Memories, and a Varied Career Started There"; and "Parker LaMoore: 1897–1954"—are detailed and forcefully written, and whose eleven letters to me (27 June; 3, 8, 9, 23 July; 1, 5 August; 9, 25 September; 1 October; and 7 November 1984) are a gold mine of appreciated information. 2) James Smorada and Lois Forest, eds., *Century of Stories: Jamestown and Stutsman County* (Jamestown, 1983), is a loving, articulate centenary tribute by dozens of Jamestown residents and friends to a distinguished pioneering community. 3) An invaluable "Scrapbook," in two unpaged binders, of L'Amour material (including original and photocopied letters from, to, and concerning L'Amour, and other informative items, some unfortunately not completely identified) assembled by Reese Hawkins, a personal friend of L'Amour, and placed on deposit at the Alfred Dickey Library, Jamestown, for the use of visiting scholars and admirers of L'Amour. And 4) happy conversations that my wife, Maureen Dowd Gale, and I had with various knowledgeable people in Jamestown on 3 and 4 June 1984.

5. Waldo, "LaMoore Family Background"; Smorada and Forest, eds., *Century of Stories*, 52–54; Klaschus, "L'Amour," 4.

6. L'Amour dedicated *Kiowa Trail* to Ambrose Freeman and also has him figure offstage in *Taggart*. From at least as early as 1958 L'Amour has been promising Jamestown correspondents that he will write a book on the Little Crow Massacre in Minnesota in 1862 and General H. H. Sibley's reprisal expedition into the Dakotas the next year. L'Amour's *Callaghen* touches on the massacre but only as an offstage event.

7. Fictional character William Tell Sackett's Civil War career, when finally revealed by L'Amour, may owe something to Abraham Dearborn. See L'Amour's "Booty for a Bad Man," 1960, reprinted in *War Party*, 1975.

8. Betty Freeman is the inspiring subject of Edna LaMoore Waldo's *Yet She Follows: The Story of Betty Freeman* (Bismarck, N.Dak.: Capital Publishing Co., 1931) and also figures in her pamphlet *The Sunbonnet Trail* (Minot, N.Dak.: *Dakota State Journal*, 1946), which has a picture of this beautiful, gentle, loyal pioneer woman, p. [4].

9. Edna LaMoore was graduated from Jamestown College in 1914, taught in several North Dakota high schools, married in 1920, was widowed in 1949, worked at the Stanford Research Institute as central files supervisor, and now lives in California. She has been a prolific and highly competent writer, lecturer, and historical and genealogical researcher. She is the author, in addition to the aforementioned works, of *Dakota* (1932; rev. ed. Caldwell, Idaho: Caxton Printers, 1936), *Leadership for Today's Clubwoman* (New York: Rugby House Publishing Co., 1939), *From Travois to Iron Rail* (New York: B. Ackerman, 1944), and many shorter works. Parker LaMoore was a veteran of World War I and World War II (to lieutenant colonel), was active in Republican party politics in Oklahoma, Ohio, and Washington, D.C.; in China was aide to General Patrick Jay Hurley, whose biography he wrote (*"Pat" Hurley: The Story of an American* [New York: Brewer, Warren, Putnam, 1932]); and then became foreign editor and chief editorial writer for the Scripps-Howard newspapers. Yale LaMoore quit high school during World War I to join the army, served in France (to sergeant), contracted pneumonia and diphtheria there, and was never well again. He became a store manager, a salesman, and an exterminator in Jamestown and Minot, and during World War II a war-plant employee in Grand Island, Nebraska, where he died shortly after the deaths at his home there of his father and mother. See Waldo, "LaMoore Family Background." Emmy Lou LaMoore was a budding, teen-aged poet— letter to me from Mrs. Rod Shindo, 9 August 1984.

10. Arturo F. Gonzalez, "Louis L'Amour: Writing High in the Bestseller Saddle," *Writer's Digest* 60 (December 1980):23–24. L'Amour once wrote a friend that he conceals his age to be more influential with young readers— Hawkins, "Scrapbook," 1. Even more odd, as it seems to me, are L'Amour's romantic, egocentric notions on aging—see Klaschus, "L'Amour," 143–45, 149.

11. John Otto was unattractive, with crossed eyes, but was adopted by his new parents, was operated on to improve his vision, accompanied the

family to Oklahoma in 1923, went on his own to California in 1926, and was later killed in an automobile accident—Smorada and Forest, eds., *Century of Stories,* 54, 160.

12. Waldo, "LaMoore Family Background." Mrs. Waldo wrote me that her father was just under six feet in height, shorter than the usual 6' 2" and 6' 3" family males because he was a twin.

13. Waldo, "LaMoore Family Background"; *Century of Stories,* 53–54; Klaschus, "L'Amour," 8; letter from Mrs. Shindo.

14. Klaschus, "L'Amour," 12, 13; Gonzalez, "L'Amour," 26. For details about the Alfred Dickey Library (in Jamestown), which L'Amour haunted as a teenager, see Smorada and Forest, eds., *Century of Stories,* 76–78.

15. Gonzalez, "L'Amour," 24, 26; John G. Hubbell, "Louis L'Amour—Storyteller of the Wild West," *Reader's Digest* 117 (July 1980):96; Michael T. Marsden, "A Conversation with Louis L'Amour," *Journal of American Culture* 2 (Winter 1980):648; Edwin McDowell, "Behind the Best Sellers," *New York Times Book Review,* 22 March 1981, 34; Sandra Widener, "The Untold Stories of Louis L'Amour: The West's Best-Selling Writer," [Denver] *Post Empire Magazine,* 13 February 1983, 10; Klaschus, "L'Amour," 13, 67; Shirley Lee, "Louis L'Amour and the Writers of the Purple Sage," *Collectibles Illustrated* 3 (January-February 1984):50. Hawkins says in "Louis L'Amour," *North Dakota Horizons* 5 (Spring 1975):14, that L'Amour "always had with him [during his years of wandering] copies of some of the series of little Blue Books published by Haldeman Julius of Gerard, Kansas. These sold for five to ten cents each." L'Amour himself says: "I am as clearly a product of libraries as anyone can be." I must add that L'Amour seems to be trying naively to create a legend out of himself when he contends, as he has done in recent interviews, that he reads eight to ten books at a time, reads a hundred books a year intensively, scans another four hundred a year, habitually reads about thirty magazines, and even studied some 15,000 books in order to select his 9,000-volume personal library—Kalter, "L'Amour," 7; Gonzalez, "L'Amour," 23; Lee, "L'Amour," 50.

16. Waldo, "LaMoore Family Background"; *Century of Stories,* 54.

17. L'Amour "packed but one change of clothes and a dozen books to take on the road"—Nuwer, "L'Amour," 99. According to Mrs. Waldo, such a statement greatly simplifies her brother's frequent revisits to his parents' homes in Oklahoma, Texas, Arizona, and Oregon—letters to me.

18. Harold E. Hinds, Jr., "Mexican and Mexican-American Images in the Western Novels of Louis L'Amour," *Latin American Literary Review* 5 (Spring-Summer 1977):129–30.

19. Gonzalez, "L'Amour," 24. For more details on L'Amour and the Far Eastern days of his youth, see Widener, "Untold Stories," 9–10. Harold Keith adds that as a seaman L'Amour went around the world in 5½ months—"Louis L'Amour: Man of the West," *Roundup* 23 (December 1975):4. Hawkins says that L'Amour "was awarded 4 Bronze Stars . . . during World War II"—

"L'Amour," 16. Mrs. Waldo wrote me that her brother did not wish to enter military service, was drafted, felt that the war would interfere with his literary career, and did not participate in the D-Day landings. But Walter A. Tompkins reports that L'Amour "was in every major action from D-Day on except the Battle of the Bulge"—"Meet Louis L'Amour," *Roundup* 2 (December 1954):3.

20. The first mention I have seen of L'Amour's autobiography appears in Widener, "Untold Stories," 10: "His publisher wants him to write his autobiography. Louis doesn't think he wants to. He hesitates a bit, trying to explain why. 'I don't like to sit here overweight, in a place where I can go up and get a damn good meal if I want to, and a good bed to sleep in. I'm not sure I could recapture the way I was or the way I thought. . . . It's hard to get those feelings back again, because I don't feel that way anymore.'" L'Amour may be charming here, but I feel he is also doubly uncandid. In the first place, his fiction shows that he can recapture poignant feelings of deprivation; and in the second place, he does like to write and talk about himself: his letters are chronically crammed with personal news. He wrote me on 18 January 1984 that he was then in the midst of writing his two-volume autobiography. Mrs. Waldo doubts that her brother, since he has so legendized himself to interviewers, will or even can write an accurate autobiography at this stage.

21. Widener, "Untold Stories," 10.

22. "Western Writer Will Be Honored," *North Dakota Motorist,* March-April 1972, 4; Jack Evans, "Louis L'Amour: The Boy from North Dakota Who Made It Big . . . Biggest . . . in the Book Writing Business," *ND REC Magazine,* July 1981, 12.

23. Wesley Laing, "Introduction" to Louis L'Amour, *Kilkenny* (Boston: Gregg Press, 1980), [xi]; Louis L'Amour, "Of Guns & Gunmen," *Gun World* 25 (September 1984):54–56. L'Amour says that he qualified in the army as expert with six different types of firearms—Hawkins, "Scrapbook," 1.

24. The name change distressed his sister, especially when it resulted in her own old name being confused with his new one—Waldo, "LaMoore Family Background"; *Century of Stories,* 54.

25. Hawkins, "Scrapbook," 1; Klaschus, "L'Amour," 14–15, 27–28. The number of skinned carcasses is now reported as 925—Hubbell, "L'Amour," 96. L'Amour's first published item appears to be a poem entitled "The Chap Worth While," which saw light in the *Jamestown Sun,* 1926, reprinted in Smorada and Forest, eds., *Century of Stories,* 189. Even back in 1926 L'Amour was romanticizing about himself: in his introduction to the poem he says that he has been wandering around the globe for the past five years—Smorada and Forest, eds., *Century of Stories,* 188. Bill Gulick, by letter to me (6 June 1984) and Savoie Lottinville, by letter to me (8 July 1984), report that their admired friend L'Amour was never a student of writing at the University of Oklahoma. L'Amour reports that at one time "I was review-

ing from two to five books every week for the Sunday *Oklahoman,* lecturing around the state and in Texas. . . ."—"The Augurin' Post," *Roundup* 18 (August 1970):10. As for L'Amour's poetry, *Smoke from This Altar* is a rightly forgotten selection of some thirty-six poems, usually short, including fifteen Italian sonnets (some irregular in rhyme scheme). The best of the poems sketch elements of nature so mountainous, stormy, and oceanic as to dwarf petty man, while the worst of the poems limn a persona who cannot be held back by transient love but must ever wander toward the vague faraway.

26. In 1951, 35,000,000 copies of Western novels were sold, or 16% of all paperbacks—Seth M. Agnew, "God's Country & the Publisher," *Saturday Review* 36 (14 March 1953):27. In 1958, eight of the top ten TV series were Westerns—"Westerns: The Six-Gun Galahad," *Time* 73 (30 March 1959):52.

27. L'Amour once voiced the opinion that if he were not a millionaire writer he could be a millionaire in any of dozens of other fields—Nuwer, "L'Amour," 102.

28. Of this pen name L'Amour writes: "I had written a series about Asia for the pulps about a character named Ponga Jim Mayo. The publisher at Standard Magazines did not believe people would buy westerns written by anyone with my name, so they wanted something 'western sounding,' whatever that is. So I pulled Jim Mayo out of the hat"—"Western Writer Will Be Honored," 4.

29. See John D. Nesbitt, "Louis L'Amour's Pseudonymous Works," *Paperback Quarterly* 3 (Fall 1980):3–4.

30. Reprinted in *War Party* (1975) and also in *Reader's Digest* 125 (September 1984):102–6.

31. See "Merchandising," *Publishers Weekly* 164 (21 November 1953):2120.

32. "The West—The Greatest Story Ever Told," *Roundup* 27 (July-August 1981):6.

33. Tom Rogers, "Author Louis L'Amour Surveys His Range," *USA Today,* 29 March 1983, 4D.

34. "About the Author," in *The Walking Drum,* [425]; Bannon, "L'Amour," 56; Bantam publicity releases. If all the L'Amours in print were stacked flat one on top of another, they would reach more than 1,100 miles into space. By 1991 or perhaps 1992, they would make it around the world at the equator if laid lengthwise end to end, given a continuation of the current rate of sales and productivity.

35. "Bantam Announces Its Plans for the Louis L'Amour Overland Express," *Publishers Weekly* 217 (9 May 1980):36.

36. "L'Amour, Louis (Dearborn)," in *Current Biography* (New York: H. W. Wilson Co., 1980), 204; Tuska and Piekarski, *Encyclopedia of Frontier and Western Fiction,* 211; Brian Garfield, *Western Film: A Complete Guide* (New York: Rawson, 1982), passim; Bantam publicity.

37. Hubbell, "L'Amour," 98. Kathy L'Amour, then twenty-two years of age, was the daughter of a real-estate developer and of an actress, and had appeared in *Gunsmoke* and *Death Valley Days* TV segments. L'Amour has revealed to interviewers that he was once engaged to a widowed French countess with two children; further, that actress Julie Newmar, to whom he was also once engaged, introduced him to Kathy. She now handles the L'Amour family correspondence, travel plans, driving, and tax details. The L'Amours are now very wealthy, own a plush Los Angeles residence, California ranch property, and two Colorado condominiums, and are participating in the slow development of a frontier-style town to be called Shalako (near Durango, Colorado). Hawkins, "Scrapbook," 1; "Louis L'Amour, Jamestown Native, Remembers Kin in Book Dedications," *North Dakota Motorist,* March-April 1972, 4; Nuwer, "L'Amour," 102; Evans, "L'Amour," 15; Widener, "Untold Stories," 12.

38. Hawkins, "Scrapbook," 1; J. D. Reed, "The Homer of the Oater," *Time* 116 (1 December 1980):107; Francis Ring, "An Interview with Louis L'Amour," *American West* 19 (July-August 1982):48; Lee, "L'Amour," 50.

39. Ned Smith, "He's No Rhinestone Cowboy," *American Airways,* April 1976, 12; Kalter, "L'Amour," 7; Gonzalez, "L'Amour," 26; Lee, "L'Amour," 50. L'Amour habitually plays host at his famous lunches to avoid incurring indebtedness to wheeler-dealers who tend to swarm about him. He regularly writes when away from Los Angeles. He once demanded that one of his Durango condos be fitted with a 250-pound barbell for his use—Jack Evans, "Authenticity in Stories Has Made L'Amour Great," *Jamestown Sun,* 1 December 1978, 11.

40. John Tuska, ed., *The American West in Fiction* (New York and Scarborough, Ontario: New American Library, 1982), 229; Widener, "Untold Stories," 14. L'Amour also avers that he "never dash[es] off a quickie"—Kalter, "L'Amour," 4. He honestly enough once confessed that he "usually doesn't have the faintest idea what's going to happen to the characters in his books. He just puts them somewhere and sees what happens"—Widener, "Untold Stories," 14.

41. Evans, "Authenticity in Stories," 11; Louis L'Amour, "Foreword" to *The Sackett Novels of Louis L'Amour,* 4 vols. (New York: Bantam, 1980), 4:vii; McDowell, "Behind the Best Sellers," 34.

42. Nuwer, "L'Amour," 99. L'Amour is regularly described as 6' 1", and 215 lbs.

43. Gonzalez, "L'Amour," 25–26. Another interviewer the same year reported that L'Amour had thirty-four plots outlined and on his desk—Reed, "Homer of the Oater," 108.

44. Ring, "An Interview," 48.

45. Gonzalez, "L'Amour," 22.

46. Tim Cahill, "The Land and Louis L'Amour," *Outlook,* February-March 1982, 29—quoted in Klaschus, "L'Amour," 196.

47. Readers interested in the legal proceedings may consult "Louis

L'Amour Sues Carroll & Graf," *Publishers Weekly* 224 (8 July 1983):20–21; John Mutter, "Judge Curbs C & G's Use of L'Amour's Short Stories," *Publishers Weekly* 224 (22 July 1983):65; Leonore Fleischer, "Black Hats, White Hats," *Publishers Weekly* 224 (5 August 1983):101.

    48. *Shalako,* [170] and later.

    49. Bannon, "L'Amour," 57.

    50. *Son of a Wanted Man,* [179]. Still later blurbs do not mention the town. See, for example, *Frontier* (New York, 1984), [215]. Earlier, it was reported in detail that the town would be constructed by L'Amour-formed Shalako Enterprises at a cost of some $30,000,000, on 1,000 to 2,000 acres of land eleven miles west of Durango, on Highway 160, with replicas of jail, livery stable, hotel, assay office, boardinghouse, office building for lawyer and physician, general store, saloons, and coal and gold mines; to be used as L'Amour movie sets; 100% authentic, with no electricity or plumbing, but instead with period artifacts, lumber, and furniture—"Novelist to Build Frontier Village," *North Dakota Motorist,* March-April 1972, 5. It is now said that environmentalists and utility companies are causing delays in the construction of Shalako.

    51. *Congressional Record* 128, no. 103 (2 August 1982), and no. 110 (12 August 1982).

    52. "L'Amour Receives Congressional Medal," *Publishers Weekly* 224 (14 October 1983):17. Retired Los Angeles and Jamestown journalist Jack Evans, more than any other person, was responsible for L'Amour's winning this award. Starting in 1978 Evans wrote and mailed more than three thousand personal letters, entirely at his own expense, to influence people in all walks of life, to stir interest in the idea—Evans, "Medal for L'Amour," *Jamestown Sun,* 18 February 1980, 4; Evans, "L'Amour Newsletter," Eldridge, N.Dak., 12 May 1980, [1–2]; "C-400 Club Program," Concordia College, Moorhead, Minn., 15 March 1983, [2]; Edwin McDowell, "Publishing: Congress Honors Louis L'Amour," *New York Times,* 23 September 1983, C20.

    53. "People," *Time* 120 (23 August 1982):61. Almost anticlimactically, L'Amour on 26 March 1984 "journeyed to the White House once again. . . . Now, he is the recipient of the government's highest civilian award, the Medal of Freedom"—so reports Jory Sherman, "Along Publishers' Row," *Roundup* 32 (May 1984):27. L'Amour may even allow himself to be talked into acting in one of his movies soon—see "A Special New Interview with Louis L'Amour," in *The Shadow Riders,* [181].

Chapter Two

    1. Gonzalez, "L'Amour," 24. The Polti book is *The Thirty-Six Dramatic Situations,* tr. Lucille Ray (1916; reprinted. Boston: Writer, 1940).

    2. Frank Gruber, *Pulp Jungle* (Los Angeles: Sherbourne Press, 1967), 184–86.

    3. Tuska, ed., "General Introduction," in *The American West in Fiction,* 3–4.

    4. John G. Cawelti, *The Six-Gun Mystique* (Bowling Green, Ohio: Bowling Green State University Popular Press, 1971), 35–67 passim.

    5. Ibid., 66–67.

    6. Ibid., 71.

    7. In *The Six-Gun Mystique* Cawelti does not discuss L'Amour, nor does he to any appreciable degree in his classic, bigger study entitled *Adventure, Mystery, and Romance: Formula Stories as Art and Popular Culture* (Chicago and London: University of Chicago Press, 1976). In the latter work he cites L'Amour in an effort to argue that the evolution of the formulary Western was slow and superficial as the 1950s gave way to the 1960s: "A western novel written by Louis L'Amour in the 1960s is somewhat franker and more graphic in the portrayal of sex [not so] and violence [not always], and perhaps somewhat more ambiguous about the moral qualities of its hero [not so]. . ." (p. 231).

    8. "General Introduction," in *The American West in Fiction,* 19.

    9. Ibid., 22.

    10. Ibid., 23. Henry W. Allen tellingly downgrades all such categorizing. See *Will Henry's West,* ed. Dale L. Walker (El Paso: Texas Western Press, 1984), especially 8–12.

    11. His particular bête noire here is Ernest Haycox's *Canyon Passage* (1945), in which, according to Tuska, Haycox was not merely inaccurate historically but also dishonest on purpose—see Tuska's "General Introduction," in *The American West in Fiction,* 15–18, 25.

    12. Rogers, "Author Louis L'Amour," 4D.

    13. *The Melville Log: A Documentary Life of Herman Melville,* ed. Jay Leyda (New York: Harcourt, Brace, & Co., 1951), 1:316.

    14. "Foreword," in *The Sackett Novels,* 1:viii.

    15. Rogers, "Author Louis L'Amour," 4D.

Chapter Three

    1. Hinds, "Mexican and Mexican-American Images," 133.

    2. Later L'Amour inaccurately calls *Hondo* his first novel—"A Letter to You from Louis L'Amour," *Waldenbooks: Booknotes,* April 1983, [1]. Bantam publicity also misstates the facts, and as recently as 1984—see *Frontier,* [215].

    3. Herbert S. Schell, in *History of South Dakota,* rev. ed. (Lincoln: University of Nebraska Press, 1968), 150, identifies the flush years of Deadwood mining as 1876–77, with the summer of 1877 being especially intense. John Milton, in *South Dakota: A Bicentennial History* (New York: W. W. Norton, 1977), 29–31, says that Jack Langrishe and his wife owned a dramatic troupe in Deadwood in 1876, and mentions Calamity Jane as well. Deadwood is

neatly if briefly sketched by L'Amour in his short story "South of Deadwood" (*Bowdrie's Law*).

4. Loren D. Estleman, in his essay entitled "The Wister Trace: A Century of Western Classics," *Roundup* 31 (May 1983):16, suggests that *Hondo* closely "parallels" Jack Schaefer's 1949 masterpiece *Shane*.

5. "Introduction" to *Hondo* (Boston: Gregg Press, 1978), ix.

6. Ibid., viii. John D. Nesbitt, in "A New Look at Two Popular Western Classics," *South Dakota Review* 18 (Spring 1980):36–39, refines Marsden's "omega point" thesis by suggesting that Hondo Lane, like his dog Sam, is tough, dominant, fast, and free, and that Angie Lowe, like a good horse, is tamable and must learn to obey. Nesbitt wryly notes that Hondo's and Angie's hearth will be on his ranch out in California, not on hers in Arizona.

7. In Oriental aesthetic terms, the background silence of the desert becomes the philosophical foreground of the noisy novel.

8. "Introduction" to *Utah Blaine* (Boston: Gregg Press, 1980), v–ix.

9. See the letter by L'Amour to Wesley Laing, after the introduction to *Kilkenny* (Boston: Gregg Press, 1980), xi. Why did L'Amour publish first the final volume of an already completed trilogy, then wait more than two decades to issue the rest? Perhaps in italicizing the world "book" L'Amour is implying that these novels were redone from earlier short stories.

10. "Introduction" to *Crossfire Trail* (Boston: Gregg Press, 1980), v–vi.

11. Tuska, ed., *The American West in Fiction,* 229, notes that he once told L'Amour "that in *Last Stand at Papago Wells* only five characters are killed during an Apache attack but one character counts six corpses. 'I'll have to go back and count them again,' L'Amour said, and smiled. It really doesn't matter [Tuska adds] to the majority of his readers and, therefore, it doesn't matter to him or to his publishers." I may add that in *Last Stand at Papago Wells* the hero is reported orphaned because "his parents died of cholera when he was fourteen" (p. 6), whereas on p. 47 we read that the hero was sixteen when his father was shot to death.

12. L'Amour makes excellent use of historical sources for details of Sitka under Russian and then American control. The last two pages of the novel mention Generals Lovell H. Rousseau and Jefferson C. Davis (Union officers, both), and the U.S.S. *Ossipee* in the bay. Two sources that L'Amour might have consulted are Hubert Howe Bancroft, *History of Alaska 1730–1885* (1886; reprint ed. New York: Antiquarian Press, 1959), 599–600; and C. L. Andrews, *The Story of Alaska* (Caldwell, Idaho: Caxton Printers, 1940), 127–28. L'Amour has his Russian flag lowered on a "morning . . . bright and clear" (p. 245), whereas in truth it was fouled and had to be cut down during a misty evening. LaBarge's old-time friend from the East, Captain Hutchins, gives aid in San Francisco; and LaBarge's tough first mate aboard the *Susquehanna* is named Barney Kohl. In real life the firm of Hutchinson, Kohl & Company made a commercial killing by buying Russian goods at the time of

the Alaskan transfer. Curiously, the manager of a commercial firm just north of San Francisco in 1836–41 was named Alexander Rotchev and sent produce to Russian Alaska. See James R. Gibson, *Imperial Russia in Frontier America: The Changing Geography of Supply of Russian America, 1784–1867* (New York: Oxford University Press, 1976), 118, 127, 129, 132, 188, 245. This book is more recent than *Sitka,* but L'Amour could have drawn on some of Gibson's extensive sources. For details of LaBarge's forgotten friend Robert J. Walker, see *Dictionary of American Biography* (New York: Charles Scribner's Sons, 1937), 19:355–58.

13. See Eugene Cunningham, *Triggernometry: A Gallery of Gunfighters . . .* (1941; reprint ed., Caldwell, Idaho: Caxton Printers, 1982), 12, 34. Nor does L'Amour seem to have consulted Ed Bartholomew's *Cullen Baker: Premier Texas Gunfighter* (Houston: Frontier Press, 1954), which, though wretchedly written, is full of information and includes a reprint of Thomas Orr's *Life of the Notorious Desperado Cullen Baker from His Childhood to His Death, with a Full Account of the Murders He Committed.* Published after L'Amour's *The First Fast Draw* was Carl W. Breihan's *Great Gunfighters of the West* (1962; reprint ed., New York: Signet, 1977), which has a reliable account of Baker (pp. 66–70); cited by Klaschus, "Louis L'Amour," 86. Klaschus's entire discussion of *The First Fast Draw* (pp. 65–66) is exemplary.

Chapter Four

1. "'All Time' Best Westerns Roster Is WWA Release," *Roundup* 25 (August 1977):10.

2. L'Amour took violent exception to criticism of *Shalako* for having an improbable cast of characters; see his rejoinder, called "An Open Letter to the Old Buckaroos," *Roundup* 11 (September-October 1963):2, 4–5.

3. These classical military authorities are very obscure. Why did L'Amour seize on their names? To parade love of the esoteric in both his hero and himself? He mentions Vegetius in *The Daybreakers* and *The Walking Drum* as well.

4. Estleman likes *High Lonesome* more than I do, but I must say that he does not offer specific evidence to warrant his general praise; see "The Wister Trace," 20.

5. If L'Amour from the start of his Sackett series had in mind twenty or more volumes, why did he name the second book to appear *Sackett?*

6. L'Amour even includes a tacky footnote (p. 149) reminding readers that Tyrel and Drusilla Sackett may be found in *"The Daybreakers,* Bantam Books, Inc."* Elsewhere, he also makes footnoted references to his own works.

7. The fisticuff adversary here is not a gun dummy, as in *Utah Blaine,* etc., but, for relevant variety, a former professional football player affectionately known as Jimbo.

8. See Cawelti, *Six-Gun Mystique,* 66–67.

9. L'Amour has a special fondness for east Texas, where the action of *Matagorda* takes place; see "Special New Interview," in *The Shadow Riders,* [182–83].

10. Any onomastic symbolism here? Hardy is the son of Scott.

11. This slip is noted in John D. Nesbitt, "Literary Convention in the Classic Western Novel," Ph.D. diss., University of California Davis, 1980, 189 n. 14.

Chapter Five

1. A wicked essay rebuking L'Amour for making Ronan Chantry a European-educated scholar "with . . . a headful of platitudes" (p. 17) is Don D. Walker's "The Scholar as Mountain Man," *Possible Sack* 4 (April 1973):16–17.

2. "Nobody ever lived who was a finer judge of horseflesh than those Irish traders"—*The Sky-Liners,* 11.

3. Was L'Amour having fun with the Hyatt House and the Howard Johnson hostelry chains when he gave one friend of Borden Chantry the name Hyatt Johnson?

4. L'Amour first described this New World Stonehenge in *Sackett,* 24–25.

5. In *The Lonesome Gods* as well, we read that the hero when he was a boy met Poe in Philadelphia.

6. Estleman notes a pair of infelicities in it, in his "Wister Trace," 20. For rollicking, critical, informative comments on both *Bendigo Shafter* and *Comstock Lode,* see John D. Nesbitt, "Reviews," *Western American Literature* 16 (Winter 1982):315–17. Nesbitt does not greatly admire L'Amour; for proof, see his parody entitled "Adventures of the Ramrod Rider, Price Ten Cents," in *Colorado State Review* n. s. 11 (Spring-Summer 1984):56–59.

7. In a 1982 interview L'Amour hinted that her Virginia plantation may attract Mary Breyton to return home one day; see *The Lonesome Gods,* [460].

8. See the review of *Ride the River* by Robert L. Gale in *Western American Literature* 19 (May 1984):66–67.

9. The resemblance is compounded for thoroughgoing L'Amour addicts by the fact that the TV version of *The Shadow Riders* starred Tom Selleck, Sam Elliott, and Jeff Osterhage as the Traven brothers, just as the TV mini-series called *The Sacketts* starred the same hirsute trio as the Sackett brothers. L'Amour seems to agree: see "Special Interview," *The Shadow Riders,* [188–89].

10. Kalter, "L'Amour," 4.

11. "A Special Interview with Louis L'Amour," in *The Lonesome Gods,* [456–57].

12. In *The Walking Drum* L'Amour effectively uses two refrains, "Your wit is a sword" and "*Yol bolsun*" (May there be a road).

13. These include frequent use of the words "loyalty," "patience," "silence," and "trouble"; vague pronoun antecedents; misplaced "only"; absence of parallelism; "who" for "which"; giveaway idioms ("taken" for "took," "There's two," "waste around"); and such images insufficiently thought through as "a strange young bull . . . who had not won his spurs" (p. 31). Further, *Son of a Wanted Man* has a time error. In *The Daybreakers,* the action of which starts in 1866, Joe Sackett is fifteen years old. In *Borden Chantry* he is murdered at the age of about thirty, hence in about 1881. We read that action in *Son of a Wanted Man* occurs a few years later, perhaps about 1885; but then we are informed that both Jesse James (1847–82) and Billy the Kid (1859–81) are still alive.

14. The final climax occurs offstage and is then narrated to us at dull secondhand. One can almost hear L'Amour apologetically telling us that he knows this ending is awkward but that he lacks time and interest to rewrite it.

15. A recent book of value for general background to the first third of *The Walking Drum* is Thomas F. Glick's *Islamic and Christian Spain in the Early Middle Ages* (Princeton: Princeton University Press, 1979). L'Amour would surely agree with Glick's thesis that "Islam's conquests . . . opened the Mediterranean, previously a Roman lake, and, by connecting it with the Indian Ocean, converted it into a route of world trade" (p. 19).

16. L'Amour goes out of his way to criticize twelfth-century Christian Europe for being intellectually stultified, theologically hidebound, and physically unsanitary.

17. L'Amour told a recent interviewer that for a traveling character "I get a big piece of paper and I lay out the point of origin and the destination. Then I fill in all along the route the character's going to travel"—Garry Abrams, "Louis L'Amour Broadens His Frontiers," *Los Angeles Times,* 30 May 1984, pt. V, p. 2.

18. For background on Sinan, one of L'Amour's most fascinating real-life characters, see Marshall G. S. Hodgson, *The Order of Assassins* ('s-Gravenshage: Mouton & Co., 1955), especially 185–99; Bernard Lewis, *The Assassins: A Radical Sect in Islam* (New York: Basic Books, 1968), 110–18; Enno Franzius, *History of the Order of Assassins* (New York: Funk & Wagnalls, 1969), 107–13. For pictures of Alamut, Sinan's formidable mountain stronghold, which Kerbouchard penetrates, see Lewis, *The Assassins,* after p. 86, and Franzius, *History of the Order of Assassins,* 41. L'Amour is au courant, since assassination is one weapon of international terrorism, now raging in the Middle East.

19. See *Fair Blows the Wind,* 265.

20. L'Amour has stated that his personal library contains twenty books on costume—Harold Keith, "Louis L'Amour," *Roundup* 24 (January 1976):9.

21. Why cannot some competent editor eliminate L'Amour's "but . . . but" and "yet . . . yet" usages, dangling modifiers, "further" for "farther," grammatical errors ("horse who," "lay" for "lie," "of we," "such as me"), "neither of" three, violations of parallelism, poor punctuation, repetitions, split infinitives, and so on?

Chapter Six

1. See interview materials in the back pages of *Comstock Lode, The Shadow Riders, The Lonesome Gods,* and *Ride the River.* On 17 August 1982 L'Amour wrote to me that he then had plans to write fifty frontier books about three families.

2. See Anthony R. Pugh's incredibly thorough book *Balzac's Recurring Characters* (Toronto: University of Toronto Press, 1974).

3. Diana Festa-McCormick, *Honoré de Balzac* (Boston: Twayne Publishers, 1979), 155. See also Mary Susan McCarthy, *Balzac and His Reader: A Study of the Creation of La Comédie Humaine* (Columbia and London: University of Missouri Press, 1982), 93, 94, 97–100.

4. Anthony Trollope, *An Autobiography* (1883; reprint ed. London: Oxford University Press, 1950), 271–73. See also Edward Wagenknecht, *Cavalcade of the English Novel* (New York: Holt, Rinehart & Winston, 1954), p. 287. Reese Hawkins wrote to me on 5 July 1984 that his friend Louis L'Amour could write anywhere and that he once saw L'Amour typing an essay at his Caliente ranch while members of his family and their guests were playing cards in the same room.

5. See Winifred Gregory Gerould and James Thayer Gerould, *A Guide to Trollope* (Princeton: Princeton University Press, 1948), 183–84, 187–88, and elsewhere.

6. For example, Ethan Sackett in *Bendigo Shafter,* Tell Sackett in *Dark Canyon,* a Sackett with no specified first name in *Chancy,* another in *The Iron Marshal,* and Packet Sackett (undeveloped) in *Milo Talon.* Sackett's Harbor (based on Sackets Harbor, New York?) is cited in *Rivers West* for no discernible reason. A late-nineteenth-century American writer as popular in his time as L'Amour is in his is Francis Marion Crawford. The two may be profitably compared as to work habits, productivity, and desire to combine romanticism and realism. Both feature historical and recurring characters, and both wrote family sagas. The narratives of each have been excellently translated into films. See John C. Moran, *An F. Marion Crawford Companion* (Westport, Conn.: Greenwood Press, 1981), especially [3]–67 passim.

7. Ada Galsworthy, "Preface" to John Galsworthy, *The Forsyte Saga* (New York: Charles Scribner's Sons, n.d.), vii.

8. See Festa-McCormick, *Balzac,* 155; F. W. J. Hemmings, *The Life and Times of Emile Zola* (New York: Charles Scribner's Sons, 1977), 69.

9. "A Special Interview with Louis L'Amour," in *Comstock Lode,* [421].

10. H. V. Marrot, *The Life and Letters of John Galsworthy* (New York: Charles Scribner's Sons, 1936), 443.

11. Ibid., 511; Alex Fréchet, *John Galsworthy: A Reassessment,* tr. Denis Mahaffey (Totowa, N.J.: Barnes & Noble Books, 1982), 67.

12. This makes highly misleading the recent Bantam advertisements offering "The Complete Sackett Saga in a Boxed Set"; see end matter in *Lonely on the Mountain* and *Yondering,* both 1980. The offer was for fifteen titles in four paperbacks for $29.95.

13. One of L'Amour's most awkward time lapses occurs between chapters 29 and 30 of this novel, when we jump from 1602, with Barnabas Sackett's children all young, to 1620, with the oldest sons mature and ready for heroic adventures themselves.

14. L'Amour oddly misidentifies Emily Sackett Talon once as Emily Talon Sackett—see "A Special Interview with Louis L'Amour," in *The Lonesome Gods,* [465].

15. Does Ethan Sackett seem a bit young to be boasting around 1860 of having known legendary John Colter (d. 1813) of the Yellowstone region?

16. "Author's Note," in *Ride the River,* 183.

17. Evidence presented here concerning the wandering nature of L'Amour's Sackett men tends to disprove Tom Sullivan's thesis in his "Westward to Stasis with Louis L'Amour," *Southwest Review* 69 (Winter 1984):78–87, to the effect that L'Amour's heroes fight to defend communities they then live in.

18. For more detailed coverage of Sackett characters, see Robert L. Gale, "Louis L'Amour's Sackett Saga: Characters & Characteristics," *Roundup* 32 (February 1984):11–17.

19. Festa-McCormick, *Balzac,* 155–56, says that critics who point out such inconsistencies are merely carping; but she manages to repeat dramatic proof of those inconsistencies herself.

20. She exaggerates, however, when she says in 1840 that any living Sackett can tell about the circa 1440 Sackett family tree.

21. Tell also twice recalls as occurring long ago his cattle work with real-life Nelson Story along the Bozeman Trail right after the Civil War, and the war itself as "a long time ago" (p. 36).

22. In an "Author's Note" preceding *Lonely on the Mountain* L'Amour promises a novel about Louis Riel and "some other aspects of Western Canadian history."

23. For details concerning Brown's Hole, see John Rolfe Burroughs, *Where the Old West Stayed Young* (1962; reprint ed. New York: Bonanza Books, n.d.).

24. For verification see Odie B. Faulk, *Dodge City: The Most Western Town of All* (New York: Oxford University Press, 1977), 157–63.

25. "Special Interview," in *The Lonesome Gods,* [465–66]. As for the original name of those who became Chantrys, I think I know what it is: it is

Larmour, a Gallic-Celtic name. In *Over on the Dry Side,* L'Amour has Owen Chantry three hundred years after the name change say that "every child of the family has known the name. But not one has spoken it aloud. And so we shall not" (p. 24).

26. Owen Chantry mentions that his great-grandfather, escaped from Ireland to England, was advised to change his name. His new name was obviously Tatton Chantry. But that was three hundred years ago. By "great-grandfather" (p. 23) Owen must mean something like his great-grandfather's great-grandfather.

27. See "Booty for a Bad Man," *The Sackett Brand,* and *The Man from the Broken Hills.*

Chapter Seven

1. L'Amour as quoted by Keith, in "Louis L'Amour," *Roundup* 24 (February 1976):5. L'Amour reads the way Mark Twain often does, like a listened-to storyteller. For example, Tell Sackett in *The Lonely Men* begins one paragraph this way: "You know how it is when . . . ?" (p. 65). The narrator of *Tucker* ends one chapter this way: "And that was how I met . . ." (p. 15). Other effective examples abound. As recently as 1983 L'Amour was still rightly recommending that good narrative literature be read aloud, so as "to hear those rolling cadences . . . [,] to hear the language, to feel the sounds" (*The Lonesome Gods,* 115–16).

2. Keith, "Louis L'Amour," 24:8–9. L'Amour's devious lawman Chick Bowdrie makes up stories the same way: "'We didn't have a name,' Bowdrie said, 'just a description. He was a horse thief who got caught and killed a man.' He was making up the story as he went along . . ." ("Where Buzzards Fly," in *Bowdrie's Law,* 30).

3. Ibid., 9. It is obvious to all discerning readers of L'Amour that he does not proofread page proofs. His works, especially the early ones, are disfigured with innumerable typos.

4. When an interviewer commented to L'Amour that he "must have quite an eye for terrain," he replied, "Yes, I do. If it happened to interest me at the time, I can describe the country beside a road I was driving along [i.e., chauffeured by his wife] 12 years ago"—"How the West Was: A Conversation with Louis L'Amour," *Frontmatter: Book News from G. K. Hall & Co.* 2 (April 1980):2.

5. It is important to note that L'Amour sees his Western heroes, based as they are upon epically stalwart pioneers in real nineteenth-century life, as positively Homeric. He has repeatedly made this clear, most recently in *The Lonesome Gods:* "This is a day for Homer [says the hero's father about 1850 in Arizona]. . . . His people were very like those around us now. Achilles or Hector would have done well as mountain men, and I think Jed Smith, Kit

Carson, or Hugh Glass would have been perfectly at home at the siege of Troy" (p. 82; see also p. 116).

6. Curiously, for a writer who stresses women in the West as he does, L'Amour is a singularly unerotic writer; in fact, he is almost Victorian in his reticence. Noting diligently, I could find only a dozen references to bosoms, for example, and half of them in *The Walking Drum,* a L'Amour novel that is unusual in many other ways as well. Profanity and obscenity are also almost nonexistent in L'Amour's works. I found only seven "God damn" usages, one "son-of-a . . ." (actually truncated thus—see *The Man from Skibbereen,* 170), and one "crap" (*The Proving Trail,* 16). One obscene villain is depicted thus: "then he cursed obscenely" ("A Ranger Rides to Town," in *Bowdrie's Law,* p. 127). Nothing worse, I assure you. The most commonly used mild profanity is "hell," employed perhaps forty or fifty times. Most such usages as the above occur in dialogue.

7. Keith, "Louis L'Amour," 24:8.

8. The first page of "Collect from a Corpse," reprinted in *The Hills of Homicide,* offers the names of eight characters.

9. "The West of the Story," *Writer's Digest* 60 (December 1980):28.

10. For beautiful photographs of playa, an agave shoot, and a yucca plant see *Frontier,* [81], [106], and [204].

11. *The Walking Drum* includes a formidable number of foreign words, mostly Arabic, many concerning food and clothing.

12. Nesbitt, in "Literary Convention in the Classic Western Novel," 192, rightly ridicules L'Amour for such lapses of "aesthetic integrity."

13. Unlike Luke Short, among other Western writers, L'Amour stresses eyes less than shoulders; nevertheless, "Grub Line Rider," reprinted in *Law of the Desert Born,* mentions eyes some twenty-six times. Ernest L. Bulow, in "Still Tall in the Saddle: Louis L'Amour's Classic Western Hero," *Possible Sack* 3 (June-July 1972):1, says that "[b]lue eyes [in Western heroes] have so long been a standard that many authors don't bother to describe them any more."

14. The world "trouble" is the most commonly used operative word in L'Amour; it appears, for example, at least ninety-two times in *Comstock Lode,* eighty-six in *Bendigo Shafter,* twelve in "Trail to Squaw Springs" (reprinted in *The Strong Shall Live*). The word "silence" appears a total of more than a hundred times in *Comstock Lode, The Shadow Riders,* and *The Lonesome Gods.* The word and the concept are also of great importance in *Frontier* (see pp. 53, 137, 152, 194). The words "lonely," "patience," and "home" are also popular. Use of the word "home" is significantly avoided in *The Walking Drum,* the hero of which seeks adventure not settlement.

15. L'Amour's best definition of a hunch comes in *The Walking Drum,* 380: "The mind gathers its grain in all fields, storing it against a time of need, then suddenly it bursts into awareness, which men call inspiration or second sight or a gift [or a hunch?]."

16. Hurting verisimilitude are two writing weaknesses in L'Amour. The first is his tin-ear use of diction inappropriately modern in fiction cast in the nineteenth-century West. For several examples, "she has a case on him," "couldn't care less," "fink," "a fun time," "got it made," "hopefully," "he is into piracy," "long gone," "we lucked out," "get the monkey off his back," "I don't know from nothing," "pack it in," "not all that much," "not that old," "I have a thing about that." The second weakness is L'Amour's occasional habit of vaguely describing, for example, a girl as "dressed as any American girl of the period would be" (*Kilrone,* 47), people as "good, God-fearing people by [their] contemporary standards" (*Reilly's Luck,* 128), and a house as "more like an eastern house than a western house at this period" (*The Man Called Noon,* 78). Why not put the reader back into the setting by direct depiction? Apropos of the unintegrated, see Don D. Walker on L'Amour's inartistic handling of source material for *Catlow,* in "Notes on the Popular Western," *Possible Sack* 3 (November 1971);11–13.

17. Walker uses a L'Amour dangling modifier as an occasion for humor: "At another point, as our hero [in *The Ferguson Rifle*] stalks the villains, the story breaks suddenly into violent action. 'Without thinking, my Ferguson came to my shoulder and I fired. One man stumbled, then fell.' In a novel in which the thinking is so shallow and fatuous, it is good to have a rifle that goes into action without even bothering to think"—"The Scholar as Mountain Man," 17.

18. This literary pretentiousness can get a writer into trouble. L'Amour, for example, writes the following in *The Lonesome Gods:* "Whatever else she was, she was certainly a woman of fine courage and no uncommon [i.e., no common] ability" (p. 222). L'Amour also uses the pretentious "That" clause to open at least three or four hundred otherwise respectable sentences, as in "That he had been marked for death on the day he rode into town, Bowdrie was well aware. That he survived the initial shoot-out had been the first thing to go wrong" ("A Ranger Rides to Town," in *Bowdrie's Law,* p. 123). Not errors, certainly, but syntactically prissy.

19. What are we to make of this? Little, I'd say. L'Amour makes nothing of the possibilities here (or elsewhere, for that matter) of contrasting pairs of heroic lives or pairs of men coming from different places or times, as Plutarch does. L'Amour does resemble the great Greek narrative historian, however, in minimizing history and stressing ethics. L'Amour is proud of encouraging people to read certain works through his having mentioned them in his writings. He wrote a Jamestown librarian once as follows: "I believe the first thing to do is to get people to read, no matter what, once they are reading, if there is any mind there at all, one book will lead them to another. I have a fine bunch of mail and cannot tell you how many people have read Plutarch because in one of my books, *To Tame a Land,* the boy who grows up to be a gunfighter read it five times [not so] . . . [sic]. I would venture to

guess judging from my mail, that several hundred people, perhaps as many thousand, have read Plutarch because I spoke of him in my books"—quoted in Hawkins, "Louis L'Amour," 14.

20. Would Ruth Mackin have been astute enough to buy and treasure a copy of *Walden* before the year 1860? It had sold wretchedly up to that date and even later. Further, *Walden* is an inappropriate book to recommend to Bendigo, who encourages majority rule and becomes town marshal.

21. Shakespeare is here wrongly noted for having "said . . . that no traveler returns" (p. 291). See *Hamlet,* act 3, sc. 1, lines 78–79 for correction.

22. See also *Chancy,* 65; *The Proving Trail,* 156–57; and *The Warrior's Path,* 29.

23. "The West—The Greatest Story Ever Told," 6.

24. These basic categories derive from Klaschus's dissertation "Louis L'Amour: The Writer as Teacher," in which Klaschus discusses in depth her subject's knowledge of general history, real-life Westerners, antiacademic bias, historical naïveté, opinions on Indians, theory of migration; his respect for the land and for natural beauty, geography and topography, ecology, Western occupations, survival techniques; the Code of the West, Western virtues, self-reliance, antiracism, a sense of Western etiquette, moderation, loneliness, goal-orientation, pride, vigilantism, aging; and attitudes regarding women's liberation, sex, marriage, and family solidarity.

25. Some of the best parts of L'Amour's *Frontier* concern little-known facts about earlier voyagers to and explorers of the New World, early colonists not only on the Eastern seaboard but also far inland, intrepid pioneers (afoot, by water, by wagon) and primitive and early settlements, Indians, early mining efforts, and gunmen.

26. In *Frontier,* L'Amour discusses the Smokies and the Blue Ridge and mentions his *To the Far Blue Mountains* (p. 59); the Outer Banks and his *Sackett's Land, To the Far Blue Mountains,* and *Fair Blows the Wind* (p. 69); the Wind River Range and *Bendigo Shafter* and *Under the Sweetwater Rim* (p. 115); and gold in bedrock and *The Empty Land* (p. 178). See also L'Amour's four forewords to *The Sackett Novels of Louis L'Amour,* especially 4:vii, repeated in part in *Frontier,* p. 156.

27. To pin it all down, L'Amour includes an awkward footnote telling us that the location is now the Mesa Verde National Park. See also *Frontier,* 159–62, and accompanying photographs taken in that park.

28. For more critical discussion on this score, see Klaschus, "Louis L'Amour," 64–82 passim.

29. In this way, as in other ways, L'Amour like Zane Grey and Ernest Haycox before him replicates what one critic calls "the Darwinian social philosophy Gray used to support his portrayal of Western life"—Gary Topping, "Zane Grey's West," 39, in *The Popular Western,* ed. Richard W. Etulain and Michael T. Marsden (Bowling Green, Ohio: Bowling Green University Popular Press, [1974]). As for Haycox, Nesbitt, in "A New Look at Two Popular

Western Classics," 34–35, rebukes his glossing over the issue of Manifest Destiny in *Bugles in the Afternoon*.

30. Michael T. Marsden has a brief comment on this inconsistency in "L'Amour, Louis (Dearborn)," *Twentieth-Century Western Writers*, ed. James Vinson (Detroit: Gale Tower, 1982), 474.

31. There is an M.A. thesis on the subject, which I have not consulted. It is Janet Faye Whiteaker, "Woman Characters in Selected Novels of Louis L'Amour," Tennessee Technological University, 1981.

32. *The Daybreakers*, 153; *Shalako*, 15. Shalako also says that he likes the idea of polygamy (p. 120).

33. See also *Mojave Crossing*: "the great courtesans of the past . . . were never passionate, loving women. They were cold, calculating. They used the emotions of men for their own purposes, they were all show, all promises. A passionate woman gets too involved for straight thinking, she becomes too emotional" (p. 87).

34. L'Amour seems to feel that fathers should treat their children as husbands should their wives. The narrator of *The Lonesome Gods* says "My father was a kind man, but he did not like disobedience or argument" (p. 42). The most erotic line in all of L'Amour comes in *Radigan*, when the young heroine longs for the hero thus: "Gretchen . . . knew she was in love with him, knew it deep in every throbbing corpuscle, knew it in her muscles and bones and in the crying need of her body, her loins yearning for the man he was" (p. 144). Tame stuff, eh, you Longarm devotees? L'Amour simplistically answered a 1984 interviewer who wondered "how come his characters never make love" as follows: "people at that time [Westerners of the nineteenth century] were more concerned with building the world than with their sex lives. Sex is a leisure occupation, and they didn't have much leisure"—Clarence Peterson, "L'Amour Detour: Western Writer Turns to the East," *Chicago Tribune*, 5 June 1984, sect. 5, p. 2.

35. Is it significant that this sweet-appearing housewife turns out to be a triple-dyed villainess?

36. It seems indisputable that L'Amour is here writing about his beloved wife, of whom he once said, "She's the perfect wife. . . . She is beautiful . . . , intelligent, reads a lot and is always busy. . . . She has a sharp business mind. She has many interests, principally her home, her children and me" —Keith, "Louis L'Amour," 24:9.

Selected Bibliography

PRIMARY SOURCES

(In order of publication. All publications, unless otherwise specified, are by Bantam Books. All reprints, indicated by second dates, are by Bantam.)

1. Novels
Westward the Tide. London: World Works, 1950; 1977.
Hondo. Greenwich, Conn.: Fawcett, 1953; 1983.
Showdown at Yellow Butte. New York: Ace, 1953; 1983.
Crossfire Trail. New York: Ace 1954; 1983.
Kilkenny. New York: Ace, 1954; 1983.
Utah Blaine. New York: Ace, 1954.
Guns of the Timberlands. New York: Jason Press, 1955; 1955.
Heller with a Gun. Greenwich, Conn.: Fawcett; 1955; 1984.
To Tame a Land. Greenwich, Conn.: Fawcett, 1955; 1984.
The Burning Hills. New York: Jason Press, 1956; 1956.
Silver Canyon. London: Bouregy & Curl, 1956; 1957.
Sitka. New York: Appleton Century Crofts, 1957; 1958.
Last Stand at Papago Wells Greenwich, Conn.: Fawcett, 1957.
The Tall Stranger. Greenwich, Conn.: Fawcett, 1957.
Radigan, 1958.
The First Fast Draw, 1959.
Taggart, 1959.
The Daybreakers, 1960.
Flint, 1960.
Sackett, 1961.
Shalako, 1962.
Killoe, 1962.
High Lonesome, 1962.
Lando, 1962.
Fallon, 1963.
How the West Was Won, 1963.
Catlow, 1963.
Dark Canyon, 1983.
Mojave Crossing, 1964.
Hanging Woman Creek, 1964.
Kiowa Trail, 1964.
The High Graders, 1965.

The Sackett Brand, 1965.
The Key-Lock Man, 1965.
The Broken Gun, 1966.
Kid Rodelo, 1966.
Mustang Man, 1966
Kilrone, 1966.
The Sky-Liners, 1967.
Matagorda, 1967.
Down the Long Hills, 1968.
Chancy, 1968.
Brionne, 1968.
The Empty Land, 1969.
The Lonely Men, 1969.
Conagher, 1969.
The Man Called Noon, 1970.
Galloway, 1970.
Reilly's Luck, 1970.
North to the Rails, 1971.
Under the Sweetwater Rim, 1971.
Tucker, 1971.
Callaghen, 1972.
Ride the Dark Trail, 1972.
Treasure Mountain, 1972.
The Ferguson Rifle, 1973.
The Man from Skibbereen, 1973.
The Quick and the Dead, 1973.
The Californios. New York: Saturday Review Press, 1974; 1974.
Sackett's Land. New York: Saturday Review Press, 1974; 1975.
Rivers West. New York: Saturday Review Press, 1975; 1975.
The Man from the Broken Hills, 1975.
Over on the Dry Side. New York: Saturday Review Press, 1975; 1976.
The Rider of Lost Creek, 1976.
To the Far Blue Mountains. New York: E. P. Dutton, 1976; 1977.
Where the Long Grass Blows, 1976.
Borden Chantry, 1977.
Fair Blows the Wind. New York: E. P. Dutton, 1978; 1978.
The Mountain Valley War, 1978.
Bendigo Shafter. New York: E. P. Dutton, 1979; 1979.
The Proving Trail, 1979.
The Iron Marshal, 1979.
The Warrior's Path, 1980.
Lonely on the Mountain, 1980.
Comstock Lode, 1981.
Milo Talon, 1981.

The Cherokee Trail, 1982.
The Shadow Riders, 1982.
The Lonesome Gods (hardbound), 1983; 1983.
Ride the River, 1983.
Son of a Wanted Man, 1984.
The Walking Drum (hardbound), 1984.

2. Short-Story Collections
War Party, 1975.
The Strong Shall Live, 1980.
Yondering, 1980.
Buckskin Run, 1981.
Bowdrie, 1983.
The Hills of Homicide, 1983.
Law of the Desert Born, 1983.
Bowdrie's Law, 1984.

3. Essay Collection
Frontier, with photographs by David Muench (hardbound), 1984.

4. Poetry Collection
Smoke from This Altar. Oklahoma City: Lusk Publishing Co., 1939.

5. Miscellaneous Items
"An Open Letter to the Old Buckaroos." *Roundup* 11 (September-October 1963):2, 4–5.
Foreword[s] to *The Sackett Novels of Louis L'Amour.* 4 vols. 1980; 1:vii–ix, 2:vii–ix, 3:vii–viii, 4:vii–viii.
Letter to Wesley Laing, 14 September 1979. In *Kilkenny.* Edited by Wesley Laing (Boston: Gregg Press, 1980), [xi].
"The West of the Story." *Writer's Digest* 60 (December 1980):27–29.
"The West—The Greatest Story Ever Told." *Roundup* 29 (July-August 1981):4–7.
"Books in Their Saddlebags: The Men Who Made the Trail." *American West* 19 (July-August 1982):46–47, 68.
"Of Guns & Gunmen." *Gun World* 25 (September 1984):54–56.

SECONDARY SOURCES

1. Bibliography
Etulain, Richard W. "Louis L'Amour." In *A Bibliographical Guide to the Study of Western American Literature,* 181–82. Lincoln: University of Nebraska Press, 1982. Lists fifteen items, is not annotated.

2. Books

Century of Stories: Jamestown and Stutsman County. Compiled and edited by James Smorada and Lois Forrest. Jamestown, N.Dak.: Fort Seward Historical Society, 1983. Contains valuable material concerning the La-Moore family.

Garfield, Brian. *Western Film: A Complete Guide.* New York: Rawson Associates, 1982. Includes valuable data on movies made from L'Amour's fiction.

"L'Amour, Louis." In *Current Biography.* Edited by Charles Moritz, 203–6. New York: H. W. Wilson Co., 1980. Standard biographical sketch of L'Amour; also discusses his ideas on writing and his historical authenticity.

Marsden, Michael T. "L'Amour, Louis (Dearborn)." In *Twentieth-Century Western Writers.* Edited by James Vinson, 471–75. Detroit: Gale Tower, 1982. Lists L'Amour's production, and discusses his geographical accuracy, use of family as theme, and depiction of women.

———. "Louis L'Amour." In *Fifty Western Writers: A Bio-Bibliographical Sourcebook.* Edited by Fred Erisman and Richard W. Etulain, 257–67. Westport, Conn.: Greenwood Press, 1982. Includes brief biography, defines major themes, and surveys significant criticism.

Tuska, Jon, and Vicki Piekarski, eds. "Louis L'Amour." In *Encyclopedia of Frontier and Western Fiction,* 208–11. New York: McGraw-Hill Book Co., 1983. Standard brief biographical commentary.

3. Articles

Gonzalez, Arturo F. "Louis L'Amour: Writing High in the Bestseller Saddle." *Writer's Digest* 60 (December 1980):22–26. Informative and useful biographical data.

Haller, Scot. "The World's Five Best-Selling Authors." *Saturday Review* 8 (19, 20 March 1981), 14–16. Places L'Amour in this list: Harold Robbins, Barbara Cartland, Irving Wallace, L'Amour, and Janet Dailey.

Hinds, Harold E., Jr. "Mexican and Mexican-American Images in the Western Novels of Louis L'Amour." *Latin American Literary Review* 5 (Spring-Summer 1977):129–41. Examines "the Mexican and Mexican-American images found in L'Amour's frontier novels."

Hubbell, John G. "Louis L'Amour—Storyseller of the Old West." *Reader's Digest* 117 (July 1980):93–98. Routine, laudatory summary sketch.

Kalter, Suzy. "Louis L'Amour: He Tells How the West Was Really Won." *Family Weekly,* 10 June 1979, 4, 7. Laudatory interview of L'Amour, stressing his knowledge of history and his writing habits.

Keith, Harold. "Louis L'Amour: Man of the West." *Roundup* 23 (December 1975):1–2, 4, 12; 24 (January 1976):8–9, 11; 24 (February 1976):4–5. Fine essay on L'Amour's early life, love of Oklahoma, his 1967 lecture at the university there on his writing techniques, and the Old West.

Marsden, Michael T. "The Concept of the Family in the Fiction of Louis
    L'Amour." *North Dakota Quarterly* 46 (Summer 1978):12–21. Concerns
    L'Amour and Indians, violence, family sagas, and his concept of the
    family.
————. "A Conversation with Louis L'Amour." *Journal of American Culture* 2
    (Winter 1980):146–58. Includes standard L'Amour self-promoting an-
    swers concerning his family, career, popularity, audience, success, and
    work habits.
Nesbitt, John D. "Change of Purpose in the Novels of Louis L'Amour."
    Western American Literature 13 (Spring 1978):65–81; reprinted in *Critical
    Essays on the Western American Novel.* Edited by William T. Pilkington,
    150–63. Boston: G. K. Hall, 1980. Divides L'Amour's production
    (overlappingly) into formulary, family, and historical.
————. "Louis L'Amour—Paper Mâché Homer?" *South Dakota Review* 19
    (Autumn 1981):37–48. Critical not only of L'Amour's post-1970
    "monomythic aspirations and claims" to become the American frontier
    Homer, but also of his simplistic treatment of character.
————. "Louis L'Amour's Pseudonymous Works." *Paperback Quarterly* 3 (Jan-
    uary/April 1981):1–12. Concerns L'Amour's works published under the
    pen names Tex Burns and Jim Mayo.
Nuwer, Hank. "Louis L'Amour: Range Writer." *Country Gentleman* 130
    (Spring 1979):99–100, 103. Melodramatically written interview of
    L'Amour, who recalls his past, early struggles, current happiness, and
    plans.
Sullivan, Tom. "Westward to Stasis with Louis L'Amour." *Southwest Review*
    69 (Winter 1984):78–87. Suggests that L'Amour's heroes often fight for
    communities that they then live in; hence his fictive movement is toward
    stasis, not a region beyond.
Widener, Sandra. "The Untold Stories of Louis L'Amour: The West's Best-
    Selling Writer." [Denver] *Post Empire Magazine,* 13 February 1983, 8–
    12, 14. Informative interview that offers material concerning L'Amour's
    youth and years in the Orient, army career, marriage and family, and
    plans.

4. Unpublished Material
Hawkins, Reese, comp. "Scrapbook." 2 vols. At Alfred Dickey Library,
    Jamestown, N.Dak. Contains original and photocopied letters from, to,
    and concerning L'Amour, and other items, including clippings.
Klaschus, Candace. "Louis L'Amour: The Writer as Teacher." Ph.D. diss.,
    University of New Mexico, 1983. Contains a great deal of biographical
    information (based partly on extensive interviews of L'Amour); discusses
    L'Amour's attitudes toward history, frontier survival, and family values.

Nesbitt, John D. "Literary Convention in the Classic Western Novel." Ph.D. diss., University of California at Davis, 1980. Contains section on L'Amour—"at once the most fascinating and the most tedious of the popular writers covered in this chapter [Ernest Haycox, Luke Short, and L'Amour]."

Index